Thank you for supporting
the YWCA.

[signature]

BREAKING GROUND:

The Daring Women of the YWCA
in the Santa Clara Valley 1905-2005

FRAN SMITH

Above: *Rubbing from the cornerstone of the original YWCA building.*
Construction began 10 years after San Jose women formed the YWCA.

empowering women
eliminating racism
ywca of Silicon Valley

YWCA OF SILICON VALLEY
375 S. Third Street
San Jose, California 95112
www.ywca-sv.org

Book design by Tracy Cox and Mignon Khargie
Copy editing by Lynne Barnes
Printed by The Press, San Jose, California

Library of Congress cataloging data:

Smith, Fran
Breaking Ground:
The Daring Women of the YWCA in the
Santa Clara Valley 1905-2005/ Fran Smith
ISBN: 0-9767007-0-0

*A handmade doll-sized Girl Reserves uniform retrieved
from a time capsule in the cornerstone of the 1926 YWCA annex.*

This book, published on the
100th anniversary of the
YWCA of Silicon Valley, is dedicated
to the women who dared to join together
to fight for justice, dignity and
a better life for all.

To the Young Women's Christian Association

What is the word on the wind today?
What is the rumor of dare and do?
Women, you came with a dream, they say,
Banded to see that the dream came true.

Women, you work for the girls that strive.
Girls on the battle-line early and late;
You are helping them keep their souls alive
As they take their chance in the fight with fate.

You are working for the unborn sister-bands,
For a great host coming the human road.
You are reaching hands to their unseen hands,
To lead the way and lighten the load.

And this be your praise as the years go by,
(And enough it will be for a soul's renown);
You opened the door when there came a cry,
You built a wall where the wall was down.

And then at the end of the ways that wind,
One joy will stay through the world's defeat,
To know as you go that you left behind
A friendly door on a friendless street.

Edwin Markham
(1852 ~ 1940)

The Benefactors of *Breaking Ground*

DATE	NAME	S
June 4 1917	Mrs. Ralph G. Cole	
	From Asilomar	Girls Cam
July 9 1917	Nathalie Wollin	
July 9 1917	Lucia L. Smith	
" "	Elsie Wright	
July 1917	Alma Dahm	
" "	Josephine Holub,	
July 9 1917	Cecile LaViolette	
" "	Alice Holub	
" "	Alice G. Rouleau	
" "	Helen Holmes	
" "	Violet Rasmussen	
	Maud Russell	
	Ida Ellen Spitler	
	Hazel Davis	
	Helen Davie	
	Irene Johnson	
" "	Ruth Martin	
	Elizabeth Hatfield	

A page from a 1917 YWCA register.

ACKNOWLEDGMENTS

S usie Wilson had the dream of documenting the history of the YWCA in the Valley. And when Susie has a dream, she makes it happen. She single-handedly raised the money to produce this book. She helped me at every step, as a source, critic and friend. As the deadline approached, she pitched in mightily to nail down details, track down photos and help check the manuscript. Yet she allowed me complete freedom to tell the story as I saw it. I am profoundly grateful for her trust.

YWCA board members, present and past, generously shared information and contacts and encouraged me with their enthusiasm for this project. Very special thanks to Helen Hayashi, Jill Arnone and Sarah Janigian for answering questions large and small and for reading drafts of the book. Sally Towse, research whiz, patiently helped untangle the mysteries of Edwin Markham's copyright and the full names of all those women on the old YW board lists. Kay Philips provided valuable perspective on the national YWCA and insightful comments on the manuscript.

The YWCA staff took time from demanding jobs to give me anything I asked for – and I asked for a lot. José Martinez, Sr. doggedly searched through the YWCA closets and crannies to unearth historical treasures. Susan Armas, Stacy Castle, Sandy Davis, Mary Diridon and Graciela Valladares showed me the work of the YWCA today. Keri McLain, Kathy Linton, Michael Snider, Robyn Peterson and LaDonna Curteman provided valuable help and showed remarkable grace and good humor in putting up with piles of boxes and scrapbooks in the office for two years.

The librarians and archivists of the California Room of the San Jose Public Library, History San Jose, the Sourriseau Academy for State and

Local History at San Jose State University, and the California History Center at DeAnza College, were unfailingly patient and helpful. History San Jose also granted access to photos in its archive as well as the collection of Leonard McKay. The Stanford University Archives provided important information on Harriet Cory and the school friends who became her YWCA co-founders. Frank Polizzi at Wagner College in Staten Island, N.Y., investigated the copyright status of Markham's poem for the YWCA. The Sophia Smith Collection at Smith College houses the archives of the National Board of the YWCA, a priceless repository on the association movement. Kara McClurken was especially helpful and generous with her time.

The local newspapers of the early 20th century offer a diligent record of civic life in San Jose. They recorded every YWCA meeting, class and board and staff appointment, and the comings and goings of the society women who led the association. Without that coverage, the first five years of the YWCA in San Jose would be largely lost to history. I relied heavily on, and quoted liberally from, papers throughout the century, particularly the San Jose Daily Mercury and the Mercury Herald from 1905 to 1930. The Mercury News archives provided important information on recent events. Thanks to Diana Stickler for providing access and research help.

I was fortunate to work with a dream team to create this book – wonderful professionals who happen to be good friends. Lynne Barnes proved to be a tough, quick, unflappable editor. Tracy Cox and Mignon Khargie got as excited as I did about all those old scrapbooks dredged up from the basement and brought vision, intelligence and storytelling magic to the design.

Thanks to Sudeshna Sen Gupta, a San Jose State student who gave up the good part of a summer vacation to provide invaluable research assistance. Thanks also to Jim Bettinger and Harry Farrell, who read the manuscript with care and shared their extensive knowledge of local history.

Without my family, this book would not have been written. My parents, Carl and Dorothy Smith, taught me what the YWCA taught so many others: what it means to be a strong woman. My daughter, Nicole, cheered me on, especially during the nights and weekends I spent working, and kept me laughing when deadline pressures got intense. My husband, David Yarnold, supported me in countless ways and I am more grateful than I can say. He is my best editor and best friend.

Fran Smith

$\mathscr{C}$ONTENTS

APPENDICES

SUSANNE WILSON

*The YWCA opened many doors for women. The key, above, unlocked the
door to Room 210 in the original YWCA building in San Jose.*

FOREWORD

I have a gold ring with the initial "R" that I wear on a chain around my neck. The ring belonged to my late dear friend, Ruthadele Sarter.

I met Ruthadele at church shortly after my family moved to San Jose in 1960. The YWCA was her cause, and before I knew it, she pulled me in. She got me to volunteer as a sewing teacher in the summer YWCA program at our church – and 43 years later, I am still volunteering for the YWCA. Ruthadele also insisted that I belonged on the board of directors – for two reasons. She had watched me work with young people, and she knew I had faith in all of them. She saw leadership qualities I did not know I had.

On the board, I met many women who shared Ruthadele's passion for the YWCA. Like her, they were strong, stubborn, humble and completely dedicated to working for a world free of inequality and hate. These women nurtured me, stretched me and opened my mind to the obstacles placed on many in our society, particularly women and children. My exposure to YWCA women at the national level – at conferences, retreats and two conventions – made me think in new ways about the possibilities for societal change. My friends and mentors challenged me to take action. I cannot imagine that I ever would have considered running for government office, if not for those experiences.

About five years ago, I learned that the YWCA in Silicon Valley would turn 100 in 2005. Women at the YWCA began talking about how to celebrate this marvelous milestone. As an avid reader of history, I knew immediately that ours had to be written. We had a story to tell that would surprise many people who never knew of the power, creativity and fierce determination of our leaders and how courageously they defied the expectations of their times. The YWCA board of directors approved the history project. Writer Fran Smith went to work.

Soon, Fran and the YW staff found a gold mine of historical material. Old scrapbooks filled with yellowed newspaper clippings, eloquent letters in fine script, dusty accounting ledgers, the cornerstones from the original Julia Morgan building and the 1926 annex, and board minutes going back to 1914 – somehow, mementoes and precious records had survived the ups and downs and moves of the years. I always thought I knew the YWCA story, but even I felt humbled and thrilled by the fascinating discoveries.

I realized that a group of about 40 prominent women in San Jose started a movement here because they dreamed of improving the lives of girls and working women. Those founders faltered, but their struggles paved the way for all of us who followed. Each generation remade the YWCA to meet the needs of the day. And each generation kept the YWCA alive despite formidable challenges.

I also realized that for 100 years, people have come to the YWCA as I did – as volunteers, club members or participants in a class – only to find their lives changed forever. The YWCA taught skills, instilled self-confidence and inspired women to reach heights beyond their wildest dreams. Most importantly, the YWCA brought women together to fight for changes in the way our society and community view and treat women and families.

This community has always strongly supported the YWCA, and the history project is no exception. Donors have underwritten the full cost of producing *Breaking Ground*. Thanks to their generosity, all proceeds from the sale of the book will benefit YWCA programs. I cannot think of a more wonderful gift for the YWCA's 100th birthday.

These days, the gold ring I wear at my neck makes me think not only of Ruthadele but also the movement she loved. The engraved "R" also signifies remembrance. And the band of gold symbolizes the powerful band of people who stand proudly with, and work tirelessly for, the YWCA of Silicon Valley.

Susanne B. Wilson

Headline from the Mercury Herald, 1926.

INTRODUCTION

K eri Procunier McLain, CEO of the YWCA of Silicon Valley, stood at the podium of the group's annual fund-raiser and made a sudden decision. Her heart pounding, she set aside her script and dis- closed a painful secret.

McLain described how she had called the YW's Rape Crisis Center near- ly a decade earlier to talk about the sexual abuse she had suffered as a child. A former nun and hospital administrator, she was a Santa Clara City Council member when she made the call, and she felt too embarrassed to give her name. In her past $4^{1}/_{2}$ years run- ning the YWCA, she had urged so many women to speak courageously, without shame, about their pri- vate nightmares. But McLain could never bring her- self to do it, until this moment, on Oct. 15, 2002.

She had listened to the stories of two YW clients: a tearful young mother in counseling for postpartum depression and a motherless 10th-grader who had found hope in an after-school program in East San Jose. And McLain had looked out at the audience of 2,000 crisply tailored professionals. According to the script, she was sup- posed to thank the speakers and ask the crowd for money. But she realized that one more story had to be told, and one more point made.

YWCA CEO Keri Procunier McLain

As she explained to the Mercury News the next day: "Whoever you are, you may also need our programs at some point in your life."

The YWCA has always operated on two planes: providing aid to the woman in need and crusading for laws, policies and social reforms to improve life for women as a whole. Although the association has changed enormously over its long history, those intermingling ideals remain at the core. The programs of the YWCA of Silicon Valley – rape counseling, teen-pregnancy prevention, education for abusive parents, even child care and support groups for new mothers – would have shocked the church ladies who founded the association in May 1905. But these programs sprang from the seeds those women planted, bearing fruit for each succeeding genera-tion and, against many odds, bringing vital sustenance to the community to this day. And that is exactly what the founders hoped to achieve.

The Young Women's Christian Association had its origins in two distinct groups formed in England in 1855. The Prayer Union sought to inspire young ladies of leisure to dedicate themselves to the Lord's word and Christian service. The equally religious but more activist General Female Training Institute worked to establish housing for nurses returning from the Crimean War. By the time they united as the YWCA in 1877, their dual ideals had crossed the Atlantic and inspired the rise of parallel movements.

Women in the teeming industrial cities of the East, working under the International Board of Women's and Young Women's Christian Associations, sought to meet the physical, educational, recreational and spiritual needs of girls who depended "on their own exertions" to make a living. In the Midwest and beyond, including in San Jose, women came together under the American Committee of the YWCA, primarily to pro-mote Bible study, prayer and missionary work. For all their differences in geography and temperament, the two groups shared the conviction that women can join together and use their collective power to create a better world. The groups merged in 1906, melding evangelistic fervor and prag-matic activism, independent spirit and top-down national structure, a pro-fessional staff and dogged reliance on volunteers, into the Young Women's Christian Associations of the United States of America.

The YWCA has always called itself not an organization, but a move-ment. YWs provided social services but did not consider them charity or treat women as passive beneficiaries. As time passed, YWs added pools and gyms, hosted summer camps and dances, and displayed a mania for crafts and calisthenics. But the association imbued these with high purpose. No mere diversions, all activities were meant to strengthen girls and women physically, intellectually, morally and spiritually, to groom the muscular vanguard of a worldwide movement for change.

The association claims an impressive list of "firsts" and a track record for groundbreaking advocacy. The YWCA established the first boardinghouse in the United States for women students, teachers and factory workers, in 1860 in New York; the first day nursery, in 1864 in Philadelphia; the first residence for unwed mothers, in 1869 in Cleveland; the first sewing-machine class, in 1872 in New York, where it also offered the first typing instruction in 1873, the year commercial typewriters hit the market. (After heatedly debating whether young women had the strength and mental stamina to spend hours pounding the keys, the YW education committee ordered applicants to undergo physical exams before taking the class, according to Mary S. Sims' 1936 history of the association. Eight girls signed up, passed the test and completed the six-month course with no casualties.) The YWCA organized the nation's first travelers' aid (Boston, 1866); first employment bureau (New York, 1872); first training school for practical nurses (Brooklyn, 1893); and first home-study courses, in 1903. All this before the YWCA of the USA even formed.

The YWCA introduced sex education in health programs (1906), held the first interracial conference in the South (1915), promoted sex education based on science (1918), supported the eight-hour workday (1920) and advocated widespread dissemination of birth control (1934). During World War II, the YWCA extended programs to Japanese Americans interned in barbed-wire camps. In 1946, it adopted an interracial charter and called for the full integration of black women in the association. In 1970, it declared its commitment to the elimination of racism and in 1976, to the empower-ment of women. Those remain the association's hallmarks.

Of course, countless girls and women came to the YWCA in San Jose or wherever they lived not to change the world, but to swim, sew, play basket-ball or make friends. They lived at the YW as San Jose State students, joined a Y-Wives club when they moved to Milpitas and enrolled their preschool-ers in YW child care when they went back to work. But even programs like these represented fresh opportunities. A residence for women students, women's athletic teams, wives' and mothers' groups – the YWCA started and inspired many aspects of community life that Silicon Valley takes for granted today.

In the late 1990s, amid turmoil in the national association, YW board women in San Jose briefly contemplated dropping the YWCA label. The notion made some sense, even without the impetus of an organizational dispute. The agency served people of all ages. It had men as clients, employees and volunteers (and as of 2004, it had men on the board of directors). The YWCA lost all religious thread long ago. Did the name, or at least the "Y," "W" and "C," reflect an archaic world view and outdated purpose? Worse, did the name convey values that clashed with the association's work in the Valley today?

As the women considered new names, however, they felt the pull and resonance of the old. Everywhere, it seemed, people felt a deep connection to the YWCA. This woman met her husband at a YWCA dance during World War II. That woman learned to cross-stitch, tango, diaper a baby, cook chicken teriyaki or fix a Ford at the YWCA. These women attended the national convention in 1970 or '76 or '85 and discovered a breathtaking sense of power and commitment to social justice. Those women stumbled into the YWCA after divorce, rape, layoff or you name it, and found the help to nudge their lives back on track. Many also found the strength to speak out and reach out to other women in need. In the end, the board stuck with YWCA. "The name really meant something," McLain said. "It meant a lot."

And it did, even from its modest beginnings, 100 years ago.

CHAPTER
ONE
1905 ~ 1909

THE PIONEERS

On the afternoon of Wednesday, May 17, 1905, about 40 women gathered in a parlor of the YMCA in San Jose and voted unanimously to establish a Young Women's Christian Association in the city.

Nobody would call these ladies firebrands. They were devout Protestants, wives and daughters of San Jose's leading men, names that appeared regularly in newspaper society columns. They wore long dresses with high lace collars clasped tightly at the throat. They addressed one another, properly, by surname, even sisters and lifelong friends. Yet in their quiet way, these misses and mesdames stepped onto a bold new path. Their association, born in fits and starts, would have a profound effect on the welfare of the community long into the future.

Before the YWCA, San Jose offered almost nothing for girls or women beyond home, school and church. No recreation center, like the YMCA's for boys. No swimming pool. No job training or help finding work. No clean, low-cost, supervised housing for a young woman passing through town or hoping to build a life in the city.

The YWCA pioneered all that and more. It also served as a training ground for generations of women, starting with that first small group. The work of creating, leading and running the association demanded skills and a measure of worldliness that few women had, or were permitted to attain. Women in 1905 could not vote in a government election – California suffrage was six years away, and national suffrage, 15. If a woman had to work – and good women weren't expected to – she might earn as little as $6 a week in a shop or factory. A woman alone could not readily rent an apartment, book a hotel room or even order dinner in a restaurant. Few proprietors welcomed a

San Jose's 1906 Independence Day parade featured mounted firemen, in the fore-ground. The triangle at back is an electric tower at Market and Santa Clara streets.

female customer without a male escort.

In this context, the vote to create the YWCA was remarkable. The founders set out to establish not another social club or men's group auxil-iary, so popular in that day. They wanted their own serious, autonomous organization. Women would develop the programs of the YWCA, determine its policies and raise money to keep it alive. They would negotiate loans, sign checks, rent space – tasks many didn't attempt even in their own households. Women would hire staff, publicize classes, attend conferences and handle a thousand other demands. Most importantly, women would devote all this energy to improve the lives of women, particularly young unmarried women at the crossroads of enormous social change.

With a population of 25,223, San Jose in 1905 was shedding its image as a freewheeling frontier town and emerging as the hub of one of the richest agricultural valleys in the world. Gambling dens and cheap vaudeville the-aters were closing. Churches and fraternal clubs flourished. More people bought homes in San Jose from 1904 to 1906 than in the previous six years, and more buildings sprang up than in the previous decade. Businesses pros-pered. And every day, girls from farming hamlets like Niles, Edenvale and Gilroy arrived at the Southern Pacific Railroad Depot downtown seeking their fortunes, or at least jobs in the shops and canneries of the city.

The Young Women's Christian Association existed, first and foremost, to keep such girls on the Lord's path or bring them to it. But the international YWCA movement turned 50 the year it reached San Jose, and it had developed a hard-edged pragmatism. A young woman needed more than Bible study to inspire Christian piety and Victorian rectitude. She also needed a place to live. She needed a job at a decent wage. She needed clean-cut companions, wholesome activities and opportunities to serve her community. The association movement, born in Britain and growing rapidly in the cities and colleges of the United States, had an ambitious agenda: to help the woman who walked through the door and to press for reforms that would expand opportunities for all women.

The founders of the San Jose YWCA took their inspiration from the pioneering associations of Britain and the United States. The group got its kickstart from Miss Harriet Cory, a teacher and daughter of one of San Jose's beloved pioneer families.

Cory was one of eight children of Sara Ann and Benjamin Cory. Her earliest influences reflected the twin ideals of the association she would organize. She inherited piety from her mother, a minister's daughter, and a trailblazing public spirit from her father, the first physician to practice in Santa Clara County. Dr. Cory was a member of California's first Legislature, the San Jose Common Council and the board of trustees at the State Normal School, now San Jose State University. Harriet attended the Normal School and in her senior year, 1886, a YWCA formed on campus. It claimed to be the first student YWCA in California, and Harriet served as its first president. After graduation, she studied at Stanford University. She later returned to the Normal School as an English instructor and YW faculty adviser.

Founder Harriet Cory

At the time, the YWCA had a more solid footing on campuses than in the general populace. By the early 1900s, hundreds of colleges and universities, including Stanford and College of the Pacific, a Methodist school in San Jose, had YWCAs, dedicated primarily to prayer and Bible study. As a faculty adviser, Cory attended annual regional YWCA conventions in Capitola. There, she glimpsed the burgeoning movement on the West Coast. She began thinking about the needs of young women who didn't attend college, or who graduated and worked, however briefly, before marriage.

YWCA members in 1907. A half-century later, Chloe Case Anderson, second from right, sent the YWCA photos and a brief account of the early years.

In the summer of 1903, Cory traveled through Scotland and Ireland, staying at YWCAs wherever she found them. The experience stirred her. In a column she wrote in the Daily Mercury two years later, she described a rainy Sabbath at the 100-bed YWCA in Glasgow. "I shall never forget how pleasant the large drawing room seemed to me with a cheerful fire in the grate, potted plants in the window seats, girls in groups talking, or apart writing letters or reading. As evening came on, they gathered about the piano and sang the same familiar hymns we sing at home, and as I joined in the singing, I realized I was among friends, for there is a kinship among Christian women the world over."

Cory envisioned such kinship in her hometown. On her return, she contacted YWCAs in Los Angeles, San Francisco and Oakland for guidance. Los Angeles, especially, excited her. Just 10 years old, it had more than 2,000 members, 13 classes, Bible study, travelers' aid and an employment bureau. Cory decided to start modestly in San Jose, with prayer meetings, a small residence and travelers' aid.

She recruited three friends from Stanford to help. Chloe Case Anderson, Laura Chapin Bailey and Beatrice French joined the first board of directors of the San Jose YWCA. Cory also enlisted women from San Jose's founding families, including her sister Edith, better known as Mrs. William G. Alexander, wife of a businessman, civic leader and longtime YMCA board member; Mrs. Alexander P. (Martha) Murgotten, whose husband published

The Pioneer, a weekly devoted to news of the Valley's Anglo settlers; and Mrs. Charles Crothers, one of the first residents of Naglee Park. The women used their considerable connections to marshal support and publicity.

Cory believed in the literal, and fairly radical, ideal of the association as a fellowship of women dedicated to mutual assistance and development. (Later generations would call it empowerment.) In her mind's eye, women of different backgrounds would come to the YWCA as equals to explore common bonds and advance common goals. However, most of the women who joined Cory and the men who endorsed the endeavor seized on a more traditional concept: the YWCA as a charitable enterprise. Well-bred, righteous ladies would raise up the less fortunate – not themselves. They would form a bulwark against evils like drink, dance and vaudeville. "A well-conducted organization of this kind would be a power for the moral, social and intellectual uplift of ... homeless girls," the Daily Mercury proclaimed in a 1905 editorial.

These differing notions of the YWCA – a band of sisters vs. a benevolent agency for those in need – both held sway. For the next century, the YWCA would straddle a double identity and struggle to stay true to two callings that often complemented but sometimes conflicted with one another. Was the YWCA a women's movement or a social service agency? Did it aim to bring together women of various classes, races and faiths as equals – or to enlist privileged ladies in service to the downtrodden? Should YWCA members set the agenda? Or should the leaders – the board and staff – determine programs and pick the causes to champion? Everyone agreed that the YWCA stood as a force for good. Would it also emerge, and survive, as a force for change?

A week after the first YWCA meeting, 30 women assembled to approve a constitution. They elected a board of directors, with Cory as chair. Through the local papers, the new board invited all Christian women to join the YWCA and help it find a home and raise money.

By September, the association had 170 members. The YW moved into a sprawling furnished house at 149 E. St. James St. and hired Annie McCormick as house secretary. Volunteers scrubbed, sewed curtains and laid sheets on 24 beds. Soon, the house had as many as 60 guests a month, most for only a night or two. "God has put his stamp of approval on the work," Cory said.

A confident board of directors approved a $3,000 budget for 1906, triple what the women had raised – and four times what they had spent – the previous year. The Home, as the women called their headquarters, hosted

The Great Earthquake of 1906 left buildings aflame at Second and San Fernando streets and caused damage throughout the Santa Clara Valley.

Monday night Bible classes, Sunday devotional meetings and frequent religious speakers, including a black educator, Hallie Brown. In late March, the YW dispatched delegates to the annual 10-day meeting of YWCAs in California and Nevada, at the Hotel Capitola. For many of the San Jose women, the conference provided their first brush with the broader association movement and innovative programs such as housing and employment bureaus. The local contingent returned in early April, determined to build a vibrant enterprise in San Jose.

At 5:12 a.m. April 18, the Great Earthquake struck the Bay Area. More than 3,000 people died and 225,000 were injured. At Agnews Insane Asylum in Santa Clara, 101 patients and 11 staff members died. In San Jose, the county Hall of Records and the new annex of the elegant Hotel Vendome collapsed. Churches, homes, schools, the main post office and swaths of downtown, especially along South Second Street, suffered extensive damage. Along with most civic and church groups, the YWCA scrambled to help.

In the days after the quake, YW women worked round-the-clock at the

Home, the hospital and the depot. The YW cobbled registries of jobs and lodging for women, and offered free beds and meals at the Home. When demand overwhelmed the place, YW women opened their own homes to the displaced.

The earthquake landed the YWCA on new, secular ground. Months after the crisis eased, the association continued to operate an employment and housing bureau. Annie McCormick became San Jose's first paid travelers' aid worker. The association formed the Indoor-Outdoor Club, the YWCA's first recreational program and the city's first club for business girls. It organized sports and picnics and limited membership to 50. Almost immediately, it had a waiting list.

But finances, never secure, tumbled after the quake. San Jose had an abundance of worthy causes but a shortage of benefactors. Young women filled the Home, but most could not pay for their bed or breakfast. In June, the association hired its first general secretary, Elizabeth Porter, a national YW administrator. But when she left four months later to tend to an ill sister in Denver, the board had no money to replace her.

Clinging to its optimism, the San Jose association registered as a charter member of the YWCA of the United States of America, established in 1906 – one of eight city YWs in California. But as demand for services grew, so did the strain. Some days, McCormick worked at the depot from 4:30 a.m. until after dark. ("Many babies and much baggage needed watching," the Daily Mercury reported.) Hiring a second matron was out of the question. Nobody knew how much longer the association could coax funds and volunteers to keep going.

And then things got worse. In June 1907, Harriet Cory, the driving force of the YWCA, announced her engagement to the Rev. R. Braun Hummel (records and newspaper accounts list his name, variously as Redelopho and Radolpho), a Presbyterian missionary in West Africa. The couple planned a simple wedding July 20 at her family's house at 435 S. Second St. (The house had survived the earthquake thanks to her father's obsession with sturdiness. He had sunk a foundation six feet into the ground, and mortised, glued and nailed every staircase tight, according to San Jose's Historic Downtown, by Lauren Miranda Gilbert and Bob Johnson.) After the wedding, the couple would leave for Cameroon, where Harriet planned to train teachers in the school established by her husband. "In leaving civilization for life among the wild African tribes, Miss Cory considers that she is merely changing her field and not her life work," the Daily Mercury said.

But her beloved association in San Jose nearly fell apart when she left.

Within months, the association suspended the employment and housing bureau and closed the Home. The YW rented four upstairs rooms in the Wilcox Building, at 97 S. First St. The women set up two bedrooms and filled the other rooms with the association's proudest possessions, including a piano, writing desk, sewing machine, cooking equipment, dishes and a 450-book library.

Chloe Anderson took over as general secretary in September 1907. She had no professional training for the job and felt hopelessly stretched. "I attempted to serve as personal counselor, employment secretary, promoter of a Sunday vesper service in the parlor, and adviser for the Business Women's Club," she recalled in a letter 50 years later. Nevertheless, in short order, she revived the jobs and housing bureau and organized weekly lectures on the Book of Job. Seven women enrolled in the course "English for foreign speakers." Fourteen women signed up for French lessons, and 26 attended Bible study. Anderson also started a current events club, the first hint of the crusading instinct that would sharpen in years to come. As she told the Daily Mercury:

"Many of us have no more idea of the events that are passing – of the history that is making – than if we lived in some isolated island of the sea. No woman can come into intelligent relationship with the world of affairs, with the men who are doing things that the world is talking about, with the problems of destiny which nations are struggling with, and not have her outlook upon life deepened and broadened."

Encouraged by the bustle in the building, the board began talking about incorporation. When the growing YW movement called for funds – as it would, frequently, over the years – San Jose stepped up. It pledged $45 to the national YWCA in 1908, including $15 earmarked for the Tokyo YWCA. San Jose pledged an additional $75 to the state association.

But the finances of the local association grew only more desperate. In late 1908, the board took a step almost unheard-of at the time: It announced plans to hit the streets to solicit funds. With the Associated Charities, a forerunner of the Community Chest and later United Way, the YWCA designated Dec. 5 as Tag-Day. Hundreds of volunteers would besiege the city, selling small red tags for 10 cents, $1, $15 and $20 to raise money for gym equipment.

From Nov. 28 through Dec. 4, women and their daughters fashioned tens of thousands of tags at "tag-tying teas" in parlors all over town. Newspapers and theaters exhorted citizens to have their dimes and dollars ready, and ministers beseeched their congregants. The Tag-Day committee marched through grammar schools and the high school, recruiting taggers. With the slogan "Work Hard for San Jose," the event became more than a fund-raiser for a struggling organization. It became a test for a community eager to shake its horse-town roots. The Daily Mercury stated the stakes baldly: San Jose had big-city ambitions. Tag-Day would prove whether it had the where-withal to pull them off.

Tag-Day was pure theater. Masked women strolled though downtown, singing. Trick bicyclists performed. From 7:30 a.m. to 9:30 p.m., children raced up to grownups and squealed at them to buy tags. The hoopla raised $2,619.15, and the Mercury exulted in the success. "It renewed patriotism and the bond of fellowship among the city's people," the paper said.

On only one score did Tag-Day fail: It did not save the YWCA.

In the fall of 1909, the association geared up for another fund-raising drive. The YW printed pledge cards, appointed committees and alerted newspapers. In a reminiscence written in 1933, Edith Cory Alexander described what happened next: "Everything was in readiness for the drive when a state [YWCA] secretary with little vision for the future, coming to aid us in our campaign, decided that San Jose was too small a city to warrant a YWCA. She persuaded a majority of the board ladies to give up the drive, which of necessity meant giving up the work of the association."

The YW ended 1909 with a deficit of $2,043. In early 1910, Irene H. Moule replaced Anderson as general secretary. After only eight weeks, Moule sent a typewritten resignation to Carolyn Patch, secretary of the state YWCA, and scribbled a rueful note: "Sometime I hope to spend a few days in a prosperous association." In July, Patch wrote to Laura Bailey, one of the San Jose founders, asking if the group had folded. Not yet, Bailey replied two weeks later, but soon. "It might as well go peacefully," Bailey wrote.

In September, the board voted to disband. The Indoor-Outdoor Club insisted on continuing, and the board handed over its membership list and treasured library. The national YWCA forbade the board from passing along the YWCA name. But the directors left their legacy.

They had demonstrated that a group of women could work together to strengthen the fiber of a modern city. They had extended the bonds of civic fellowship to people who had traditionally been left out – or, at least, side-lined to brew tea and bake gingersnaps for the men who did the important work. The YWCA had shown that women could be part of the lifeblood of a thriving community. As its last act, the board publicly urged the citizens of San Jose "to continue their support for the work of young women."

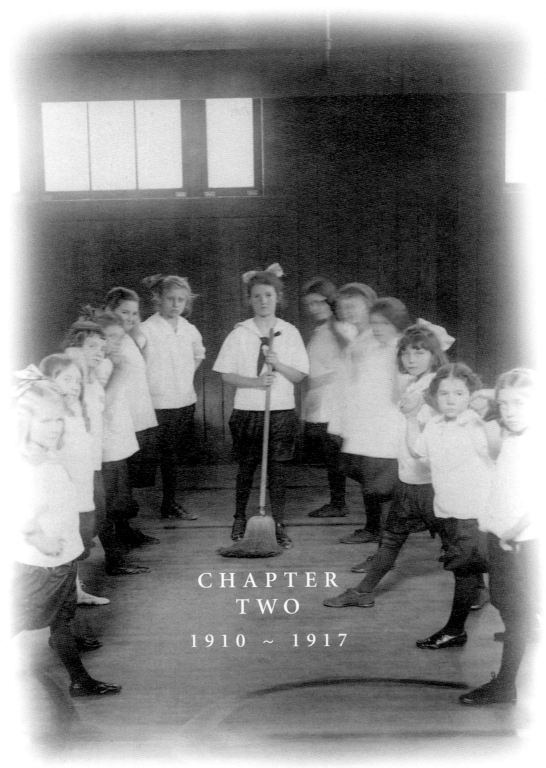

CHAPTER TWO

1910 ~ 1917

BORN AGAIN

J ust as the YWCA shut down in San Jose, it took off in the rest of California. Pasadena, Redlands, San Bernardino – YWs formed in even the sleepiest cities. The annual regional meeting outgrew the Hotel Capitola. In 1912, philanthropist Phoebe Apperson Hearst hosted the conference at her Livermore estate, a turning point for the state and national movement.

Hearst hired workers to build a tent city in a hillside oak grove overlooking her hacienda. She hired the steward of San Francisco's exclusive (and all-male) Bohemian Club to supervise the kitchen. Three hundred delegates arrived to find carpeted platform tents, hot-water baths and cots with horsehair mattresses. After a sudden rainstorm, the women also found 300 pairs of boots and umbrellas. "This camp is surely a marvel," Grace H. Dodge, the first president of the national YWCA, wrote to New York headquarters.

Hearst resolved to find a permanent conference site for the national association. She traveled the coast and chose a serene 30-acre tract with pine forests and sand dunes near Pacific Grove. Hearst negotiated with the Pacific Improvement Co. to donate the land and contributed the camp equipment on her estate. She hired a young architect named Julia Morgan, who designed the buildings of what came to be called Asilomar from 1913 to 1928. By then, Morgan had completed hundreds of commissions, most famously Hearst Castle, home of Phoebe's son, William Randolph Hearst.

Philanthropist Phoebe Apperson Hearst

Morgan had a loyal following among Christians like Phoebe Hearst and her YWCA friends. They believed in human perfectibility and cherished the idea that a flawless, beautiful building not only pleased the eye but also inspired the soul. In Morgan's clean designs and attention to detail, clients saw the physical representation of their spiritual ideal. She became a kind of house architect for the YWCA in the West, designing buildings in Honolulu, Fresno, Riverside, Boise, Pasadena, Oakland and San Francisco. In 1915, she designed the three-story building that resurrected the YWCA in San Jose.

Hundreds of people worked feverishly to establish the new YW. But like the original, it owed its start to one strong woman. Maria P. Schofield was born in 1836 in Milwaukee. A pioneer settler in the Union district of the Santa Clara Valley, near the San Jose-Los Gatos border, she worked as one of the first schoolteachers in California. She quit teaching to marry rancher Christopher Schofield. They had no children, but she never lost her interest in education or the welfare of the young.

Architect
Julia Morgan

The couple donated an acre to the Union School District to build its first permanent schoolhouse. (Chris Schofield required that the district build a "hog-tight fence" around the property and dig a well deep enough to guarantee cool, sweet water for the children.) Maria and other farm wives organized We and Our Neighbors Club, where they gathered, sewed and gossiped. A member donated land on Los Gatos-Almaden Road, and Maria paid to build a clubhouse. The club was still meeting there in 2005.

After her husband's death in July 1909, Schofield moved in with a cousin in Niles, now part of Fremont. In 1911, Charles G. Titus came calling on behalf of the San Jose YMCA, which was raising money for a building on Third and Santa Clara streets. (As he later wrote to

Benefactor
Maria Schofield

Carolyn Patch, head of the state YWCA, Schofield had inherited her husband's money "and under the grace of God she is giving it away. Believe me, I will help her get rid of it just as long as I can.") Schofield donated $25,000 to the YMCA and began telling friends she wanted to make a similar gift for young women.

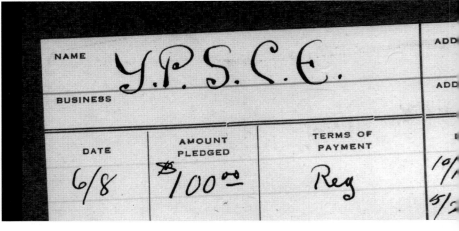

A ledger recorded payments made on pledges received during the 1914 fund-raising

The local Women's Christian Temperance Union wasted no time, telling Schofield it would build a home for wayward girls if she would pay. She wrote to Titus to ask his opinion. He visited immediately and insisted that the YWCA, not the WCTU, had the track record for helping and housing girls. Then he wrote Patch: "This is a chance for the YWCA to get on the map of San Jose."

For months, both groups vied for Schofield's money. She wavered, in torment. The Temperance Union had been active in the Valley since 1855, and Schofield, a teetotaler, felt deep allegiance. But she feared she would end up bankrolling the entire project. "That would require more means than I have to spare," she confessed in a letter to Lillian E. Janes, general secretary of the Pacific Coast Field Committee of the national YWCA.

Schofield admired the YW's work with girls but not its Christian fervor. "It is, in a way, a church organization," she told Janes. "I am, myself, one of those who believe there are too many churches in the country." She also hesitated to invest in an association that had already stumbled in San Jose.

Janes promised that if Schofield pledged $25,000, the YWCA would raise $75,000 more to build and furnish a residence and community center for women. Schofield eventually agreed, with a condition: "that the WCTU shall have *free* use *always* of the assembly hall in the building for their regular meetings." (According to YWCA lore, Schofield specified that no alcohol ever be served in the building. The association files contain no such request, since the sober ladies who founded the YW would not have

First Presbyterian Church
C. I. Griffin Treas.

AMOUNT RECEIVED	VISITOR	REMARKS
25⁰⁰	Grace Mason	1780
25⁰⁰		3/5/

blitz for the original building. The campaign raised $105,310.

dreamed of permitting devil drink. Nevertheless, the unwritten ban lasted for the 57 years the building stood.)

In late 1912, Schofield deposited $25,000 in escrow and sent Janes the names of "important men" who might aid fund-raising. But first, the new YW had to reckon with the old board. Some of its members continued to meet as a quasi-YWCA under the aegis of the Indoor-Outdoor Club. Schofield suggested including them in the new venture so they wouldn't sabotage it. "Women are so touchy," she wrote. Janes, however, insisted on all fresh faces.

Janes never outright asked the old directors to keep away. She also shrewdly didn't mention Schofield's gift. Instead, she told them of the Field Committee's interest in San Jose and urged them to do what they thought best for the continued work of the YWCA. The former board met March 4, 1913, and again declared itself disbanded. That evening, Mrs. E.W. (Maud) Jack wrote to Janes: "We are entirely free from debt, and leave to your committee our charter, our good-will and a clear field."

Jane Neill Scott, a YWCA organizer, arrived a few weeks later to lay the groundwork for a building drive. She considered San Jose a "peculiar beast" where national YWCA programs, such as training for factory girls, would be "entirely without fruit." Yet she saw an urgent need. As she reported to the Field Committee: "It is possible to gather a hundred young girls off the streets almost any night between 10 and 11 o'clock. The town is absolutely without any organization the primary purpose of which is to centralize and conserve the life of its women. Suffice it to say that the agents of vice seem unusually alert and appallingly successful in filling up the spare time of girls who yield to their allurements just because nothing else is offered them."

The YWCA had never attempted a project like San Jose's. The Blue Triangle, the insignia modeled on the YMCA's red triangle whose sides symbolized body, mind and spirit, was popping up on buildings around the country. These buildings brought recognition and stability to the national YW movement — but they represented the dreams and sweat of local women. In San Jose, by contrast, the national YW had just gotten rid of the last local members and now drove the effort to start over, beginning with new headquarters.

Still, the project needed community champions. Scott and Janes enlisted a cadre of women. Like the 1905 founders, the new YW group came from pioneer stock and the educated upper crust. Members included Ruth Laird Kimball, dean of girls at San Jose High School, the only high school in the city; Mrs. Arthur (Jessica) Washburn, who operated the Washburn preparatory school; and Frances Schallenberger, whose father, Moses, had traveled overland to California in 1844, in the first wagon party over the Sierra.

San Jose's Urgent Need
$100,000 for a Building for Young Women

WHY—
    The Garden City is the center of the richest valley in the world. Girls and young women constantly come here from the surrounding towns and farming districts.
    As a near neighbor to the second port of entry in the United States, San Jose must be prepared to receive her share of the numbers of girls and women who will come here in 1915.
    San Jose has made provision for many public needs, but thus far she has done nothing adequate for her young women.
    San Jose is the only city of her size on the Pacific Coast without a well equipped Young Women's Christian Association.

WHEN—NOW.
    The need for a modern organization and building has existed for some time. The unusual problems of the Exposition year make this need urgent.
    The boys and young men have their center for play, games, swimming and gymnasium. Where is the recreational center for the young women?

YWCA ARCHIVES

A pamphlet to encourage donations played on the conscience of San Jose.

The Young Women's Christian Association in Santa Clara Valley incorporated May 15, 1914, with Mrs. David A. (Agnes) Beattie as president, a 12-woman board of directors and headquarters at the Garden City Bank at First and San Fernando streets. San Jose sent seven delegates to the YWCA regional meeting at Asilomar (a name credited to a Stanford student, who melded together Spanish for refuge – *asil* – and sea – *mar*). The board affiliated with the YWCA of the USA in September, and named an advisory council of influential men. (The advisory group would provide critical, at times lifesaving, help through the years; it added women in 1968. Not until 2004, however, did the YW add men to the board of directors.)

The YWCA declared a single goal: to raise $100,000 for a building. (The association did not announce Schofield's gift until the official campaign kickoff.) Kimball chaired the building committee, overseeing design and construction. State Sen. Frank H. Benson, a Republican and Progressive, headed the fund-raising.

The building drive attracted prominent supporters who became YWCA angels for decades to come. Attorney Herbert C. Jones provided legal and financial guidance for the rest of his life; he helped save the YW from bankruptcy after the Depression and from the San Jose Redevelopment Agency in the early '70s. Probably the most important person to sign on was John D. Crummey, a devout Methodist, teetotaler and Sunday school teacher. His grandfather had started the Bean Spray Pump Co., which mechanized and thereby revolutionized insecticide use in orchards. Crummey inherited the firm and turned it into one of the world's largest producers of power spraying equipment. He later expanded into automated food processing equipment and renamed the company the Food Machinery Corp. During World War II, he shortened the name to FMC and made a fortune manufacturing tanks.

He and his two wives, Vivan, who died in 1951, and Caroline, a Methodist bishop's daughter whom he married in 1952, donated generously to the YWCA and for years hosted teas, club picnics and the annual Aquacade, a swimming exhibition and fund-raiser, at the Crummey estate in the Rose Garden. Both women served on YWCA committees almost to the day they died, although Caroline resigned as a director during the politically tumultuous 1970s.

Ten percent of San Jose's population earned buttons by pledging.

The 10-day YWCA building campaign started June 2, 1914. Volunteers hung a giant "clock" sign on the First National Bank, the minute hand measuring mounting pledges. Scores of people gathered downtown each morning to hear rousing speeches before fanning out on foot, bicycle and even a few motorcars. At age 78, an intrepid Maria Schofield rode shotgun with a volunteer who had little fund-raising experience and even less driving aptitude. The two ladies drove through plowed fields, ditches and grassy hillsides, determined not to overlook a single home.

The campaign played to the religious devotion, moral anxieties and civic

Crowds swelled and tension mounted as the donation "clock" recorded pledges.

insecurities of the populace. Volunteers distributed small blue prayer cards, with a divine appeal "that the men and women be awakened to see the need" for a YWCA ("If ye seek, I will do." – John 14:14). A pamphlet on glossy ivory-colored paper described the YW as the progressive, feminine counterpart to the YMCA: "Girls need wholesome recreation and sturdy friendships as much as boys do." Girls also apparently needed moral protection. A brochure warned: "It is better to prevent than to punish. It is better to form character than to reform it." The brochure noted that San Jose needed this feather in its civic cap. "San Jose is the only city of its size on the Pacific Coast without such an organization for girls and women."

The pledges shot up and then stalled. The campaign entered the final day with $86,144, leaving the volunteers to raise nearly $14,000 – more than they had collected in any single day. A somber crowd gathered. Charles Titus stepped forward to speak. After the YMCA campaign three years earlier, he had called San Jose the toughest city he had ever organized because of indifference and lack of self-confidence, according to *The Hundred Year*

History of YMCA in San Jose and Santa Clara Valley, by Levi Gilbert. Now, Titus blasted the apathy that threatened to doom the YWCA. Failure "would be a lasting disgrace," he thundered.

"It would be the hardest blow that the city has ever received and would cast a cloud which would not pass over for many years," he warned. "I don't know of a place in the world where there is more money to the square foot than there is in San Jose, and it is simply unthinkable that the citizens would allow this campaign to fail."

By noon, the sign on the bank registered $96,000. People began milling outside the YWCA headquarters. At nightfall, the crowd swelled to 500. According to newspaper accounts, Benson handed a slip of paper to Schofield, who read the tally: $105,310. "San Jose will be a better city for what you have done in the last 10 days," she cried out, tears streaming.

Three thousand people had pledged money to the YWCA, one of every 10 residents of San Jose. The women of the board reveled not only in their success but also in a newfound confidence and sense of competence. In his 1922 history of Santa Clara County, Eugene T. Sawyer wrote: "The expert work of the national YWCA secretaries was a revelation to the workers in San Jose, who had not before realized that women could be so efficient and far-seeing."

The association purchased the southeast lot on Second and San Antonio streets for $27,500; the group paid $20,000, and donors and nearby property owners covered the rest. The YW hired Julia Morgan for $3,600. The association laid the cornerstone at 5 p.m. Oct. 1, 1915, in a huge celebration. Edwin Markham, an internationally acclaimed poet and graduate of San Jose Normal, read a piece he had written for the cornerstone ceremony of the national YWCA headquarters, built in Manhattan in 1912.

> *Women, you work for the girls that strive.*
> *Girls on the battle-line early and late;*
> *You are helping them keep their souls alive*
> *As they take their chance in the fight with fate.*

The Blue Triangle opened Friday evening, May 12, 1916, with a reception for the board, the advisory council, the workers and builders. Stanford President Ray Lyman Wilbur spoke at the religious dedication that Sunday. (Theresa Wilbur Paist, his sister, was an organizer and early staff member of the national YW, and would serve as president of the YWCA of the USA in the 1920s.) The following week, the YWCA hosted teas or musicales daily at

3 and at 8 p.m., each for an influential group: newspaper and professional men, civic and commercial clubs, church and philanthropic societies, club-women, fraternal societies, county officials. Girls attended the final reception Saturday night and danced around a maypole.

Newspapers called the building beautiful. Sawyer praised it as a "lasting monument to the vision and good people of San Jose." As it happened, the YW would outgrow it by the mid-1920s. But it was easy to understand the excitement of the moment.

The building had three stories plus a basement. There was a 40-foot by 60-foot gymnasium, showers, dressing rooms and a pool, San Jose's first for women. There were 16 bedrooms to accommodate 22 women, and offices, parlors, a sewing room and an upstairs cafeteria. The third floor had an expansive assembly room with a stage and a magnificent redwood-beamed ceiling, classic Julia Morgan. The room was named Schofield Hall.

The $78,000 project left the fledgling association strapped for cash – $30,000 in outstanding pledges had not been paid by opening day and only $2,000 remained on hand for furnishings. An elevator shaft stood empty because the YW had no money to install a lift. But if the Young Women's Christian Association was meant to be a movement, not simply a building, San Jose's opened stronger than anyone expected. It listed 3,100 charter members, well over its goal of 2,000, ranging in age from 10 to 94-year-old Mary Cary.

Ada B. Hillman became general secretary, at a salary of $110 a month. Mary Bolan was the first physical director and Mrs. G.E. (Sarah) Shearer, the first housemother. The pool, under a large skylight, was heated to 70 degrees and guaranteed "hygienic." (The YW billed it "The Pool for Fastidious Folk.") It posted designated hours for business girls, college students and girls under 16 – and it was packed. A dip cost 30 cents for adults and 25 cents for girls. The installation of an electric hair dryer made headlines.

A Bible study group met weekly. A series of informal talks covered topics such as "Cooperation" and "The Contagion of Friendliness." The Tuesday Evening Club, geared to working women, served supper followed by swimming or exercise. The Silver Links Club recruited seventh- and eighth-graders who had to promise to exercise and learn something new every day, as well as to be happy and "pure." In the fall of 1916, the board voted to organize a Bible class for "colored girls" and accept them for membership.

The building became San Jose's first community hub for women. Groups including the Young Women's and Monday clubs rented meeting rooms for

The YWCA building on Second and San Antonio streets, designed by Julia Morgan, was San Jose's first community and recreation center for women.

$1.50 to $2 a month. The WCTU, of course, met in Schofield Hall for free.

In keeping with national rules, only women who belonged to evangelical Protestant churches qualified for YWCA voting membership and board service. Although any woman could join as a non-voting associate, register for classes or book a bed overnight, the YWCA of the early 20th century was a Protestant enterprise, closely tied to the revival movements that had swept the country since the mid-1800s. In September 1916, when Dr. William

YWCA parlors offered women, shown in 1916, a tranquil refuge.

Edward Biederwolf brought his evangelical campaign to San Jose, its five-member central women's committee included three YW directors. They helped deliver thousands of people to Biederwolf's makeshift tabernacle. Ada Hillman escorted a Biederwolf emissary to the canneries for noon prayer meetings.

With an impressive building, the board and staff began 1917 determined to keep the YWCA humming. It held teas for prospective members and organized a millinery class, a choral group and an elevator fund. (The need for cash, however, did not trump principle. When a young musician named Maud Caldwell offered to give a recital to raise funds for the elevator, the directors refused, insisting that entertainment must feed the soul, not the till.) Daily front-page headlines blared news of the fighting in Europe, but if the women worried about it, they didn't consider it an issue for the YWCA. The board minutes of 1916 through the early spring of 1917 allude to the war only once, when white swimsuits had to be ordered instead of blue because of a "famine of dyes."

In April, the United States entered the war. Patriotic fever gripped the nation. Thousands of people marched in downtown San Jose to demonstrate support. And almost overnight, the YWCA found a new calling.

CHAPTER
THREE

1917 ~ 1929

DREAMING BIG

The YWCA, locally and nationally, leaped to prominence on the home front of the Great War. In 1917, the federal government tapped the national YWCA to participate in the United War Work Campaign, making it the only women's group in the consortium of seven organizations charged with organizing relief efforts. Volunteers and donations streamed in, transforming a young, struggling association into a household name, a multimillion-dollar enterprise and a powerful force across the country.

The national YWCA announced huge fund-raising goals, then set ambitious quotas for locals. In October 1917, National pledged to raise $1 million, with the Santa Clara Valley to contribute $3,300 – half its budget for the year. In December, National launched a $4 million drive to establish rest centers for nurses at the front and improve conditions in munitions factories employing women. San Jose agreed to raise an astronomical $16,000. Few believed the YW could pull it off, least of all the board members who led the drive, Mrs. Lou T. (Iva) Smith and Agnes Beattie, according to a wartime history by journalist Edith Daley. In 10 days, though, the campaign collected $20,000.

Women throughout history had responded to the calls of war, sending their men to battle, bandaging the wounded and comforting the bereaved. But never before did women play a central role in rallying public support and raising funds. The success of the local YWCA campaigns of 1917 led to the formation of the Women's Mobilized Army of Santa Clara County, with Smith as colonel, Beattie as lieutenant colonel, Schofield Hall as base and hundreds of women as foot soldiers. They divided the county into precincts and the city into districts and marched door-to-door serving every patriot-

The 1920s were a time of growth for the YWCA, which expanded its headquarters. Above: Girls rumble by the new annex.

ic campaign: Liberty Bonds, Thrift Stamps, food collections, flag sales, Red Cross drives.

The YWCA war effort, however, went well beyond soliciting the citizenry. Hundreds of thousands of servicemen were pouring into American cities. Some brought wives and girlfriends; others left their women behind. Either way, the YWCA stood ready to help. The YWCA National Board opened Hostess Houses at military camps around the country, where a woman visiting a serviceman could find a bed, a proper meal, a chaperone if necessary and a dose of feminine cheer. YW women in San Jose volunteered at the Hostess House at Camp Fremont, in what is now Menlo Park. (Julia Morgan designed the spacious building, which later was moved to Palo Alto and eventually housed MacArthur Park restaurant.)

The YWCA also invited soldiers to San Jose. Board members hosted ice cream socials in their homes and parlor parties in the building. These featured charades, choral performances and group singing – but not dancing, which the board considered improper. In 1918, the business girls, enthusiastic participants at these gatherings, asked the board to drop the ban. The

More than 200 Girl Reserves formed a white triangle at the YWCA national

board split indecisively until the spring of 1919, when it voted to allow chaperoned dances.

The YWCA took pride in its efforts to give servicemen a taste of home. But the intent was not strictly to boost the morale of lonely men; the YW also wanted to protect the morality of young women. YWCA leaders regarded military camps as swamps of sin and syphilis. By that view, Hostess Houses and supervised parlor games served as community safeguards, though no doubt the business girls who attended the parties didn't see their mission

conference center at Asilomar in 1926.

quite that way.

The association continued traditional clubs and classes throughout the war, with a martial tinge. In 1918, the YWCA of the USA organized the Girl Reserves to bring 12- to 18-year-olds into the national movement, with sailor-style uniforms and three-fingered salutes. The San Jose YW formed Girl Reserves groups at San Jose High and in junior high grades. The timing proved fortunate. When the deadly influenza epidemic of 1918 forced the closure of schools (and all public gatherings, including YWCA parties),

Wartime workers gathered in a YWCA parlor in New York City in 1918.

the Girl Reserves stayed busy hiking in Alum Rock Park and along Monterey Road.

Like the national association, the YWCA in San Jose emerged from the war richer, bolder and more credible. Religion continued as the central purpose, and service remained the main objective. But subtly, and largely prodded by National, the San Jose YW took a stronger interest in the social and economic movements of the day – particularly labor, an unpopular cause as any among the Valley's leading men.

Emma Palmer, San Jose's general secretary from 1919 to 1923, embodied the new YW spirit. Palmer had studied industrial welfare at the University of California and worked at the Hercules powder plant in Contra Costa County during the war. After the November 1918 armistice, National sent her to San Jose to set up a model project: a lunchtime lounge for women in the canneries.

With seed money from the national office, Palmer established the Industrial Center in a converted bottling shed and cottage on Fourth and Lewis streets. In canning season, about 150 women a day came for a hot lunch, chat or simply a chair. That must have seemed quite the luxury, since before the center opened, women had to eat in empty freight cars or warehouses. Midway through the second season, the funds from National ran out. Palmer tried to persuade cannery owners to pick up the costs but

Thousands crowded San Jose streets in 1919 to welcome home their doughboys.

failed. The lounge closed. The venture, however, brought labor issues to the attention of the San Jose YW directors – many of them wives and daughters of fiercely anti-union growers, canners and bankers. Before long, the board was writing impassioned letters to lawmakers and editors, urging passage of minimum-wage laws for women and child labor protections.

The growing activism of the board was hardly surprising, given the political currents of the day. The YWCA nationally was a child of the Progressive Movement. But only after the ratification of the 19th Amendment in 1920, guaranteeing them the constitutional right to vote, did women count as grownups in the political mainstream. The association did not lead the suffrage battle, but the group helped women take full advantage of the triumph. In 1920, the San Jose YW offered a course in the rights and responsibilities of citizenship. Classes covered world democracy, social thinking and striking a balance between self and society – a topic summed up by a newspaper this way: Respect differences of opinion. Remember that a cool head makes good logic. Don't lose your temper, and if you do, keep your mouth shut.

The association ran a country refuge for working women, Farwell Cottage in Saratoga. Located on the former homestead of Jennie Farwell and her brother Franklin, early settlers and civic leaders, the cottage doubled as a retreat for the YW board and staff.

All of San Jose society turned out at the Hotel Vendome in April 1925, when the YWCA launched a campaign to raise $125,000 for an annex.

The YW also played a growing role in San Jose civic affairs. In 1922, it spearheaded the Reciprocity Lunch, a monthly gathering of women representing 15 Protestant churches. It met for at least 18 years, chaired by a YWCA director. It never stated a clear mission but the group managed to get its way on issues the women cared about. In May 1926, the Reciprocity Lunch organized the first public forum on the awful conditions at the county juvenile detention center, in the basement of the Hall of Justice. Newspapers published accounts of the meeting along with photos of a filthy washroom, crumbling walls and an airless, decrepit bedroom, stirring a community outcry and, eventually, reforms.

In 1923, the YWCA participated in one of the most enduring community ventures: the founding of the Community Chest. YW women wrote the early brochures for the group, a forerunner of United Way, and helped sell the controversial concept of centralized fund-raising for charitable and social service organizations. The women also knocked on doors, collecting money. The YWCA was amply rewarded for its support: It received $1,170.91 in the Chest's first-year allocation, second only to the Good Cheer Health Center.

Like the city around it, the YWCA grew quickly after the war. Board members began grumbling about their headquarters. They wanted a bigger residence and a ground-floor cafeteria to attract foot traffic – both impossible in the three-story building. In 1920, when the owner of the adjoining lot offered to sell for $12,850, the board grabbed it. The association paid $5,000 and took a deed of trust for the rest.

With land for expansion, the directors no longer griped privately about the building. They complained publicly. Beattie, now chair of the building committee, criticized the "nearsighted" folks who had erected a 22-bed residence, when 250 beds were needed. (So much for the "lasting monument to the vision" of San Jose, or Beattie's once-proud role in the 1914 fund-raising campaign.) Even General Secretary Palmer called the YWCA "a parasite" on the community, stuck in a building too small to support itself and reliant on the public's largesse.

In 1922, '23 and '24, the board laid plans for fund-raising to build an annex, then scrapped them for various reasons: bad crops after record-cold winters, bad crops after record rainfall, competing campaigns and the like. In 1924, the association could not raise enough cash even to pay the debt on the lot: A carnival to raise $3,000 earned only $1,000, forcing the association to borrow even more. That disappointment hinted at troubles ahead, but YW women did not seem to notice.

Supporter and adviser John D. Crummey

And who can blame them? Despite the on-and-off again local economy, the city enjoyed a buoyant optimism in the 1920s, accompanied by a growth spurt. Downtown seemed, literally, to spring from the ground, in a construction frenzy that would not be repeated until the 1980s. A.P. Giannini's Bank of Italy tower, the Trinkler Dohrmann and Medico-Dental buildings, the Ryland and Garden City bank additions, the million-dollar Sainte Claire Hotel, said to offer the most luxurious lodging between San

Splendidly Equipped Building of San Jose Y. W. C. A.

IT IS doing good work, it has a lofty ideal of service to guide it, we know. But many of u- are not familiar with the origin of the Young Women's Christian association, an organizaoion that is working for the betterment of wo- manhood in 47 countries of the world. Of these 47 countries, 20 have national organizations like ours in the United States which is the parent association.

Back in March, 1866, 30 ladies met at the home of Mrs. Henry F. Du- rant in Boston, and adopted a con- stitution for an association, whose object was the "temporal, moral, and religious welfare of young women

employment bureau, assembly hall, gymnasium, offices of administra- tion, parlor and reading rooms, large dining room and sleeping rooms for 156 girls. In 1868 and 1869 Women's Christian associations were formed in Cleveland and Cincinnati, Ohio and St. Louis, and places of "safety" for young women thrown on their own maintenance," were opened.

Under a still further variety of circumstances did the other pioneer associations come into being. Al- most every one of the pioneer asso- ciations started some work which later became a prominent independ- ent philanthropy in the city. Ex- amples of this are the Women's Exchanges for the sale of women's handiwork which the Women's Christian association of Cincinnati

that time the organizations have been constantly appearing in all the larger cities of our country, and of the world too, for the leaders of this movement realized that what was good for the women of one country was for the good of theirs. In 1906 the two existing organiza- tions—The International committee of the Women's and Young Wo- men's Christian associations and the America committee—were united, to form the national board of the Young Women's Christian associa- tion of the United States of Amer- ica, the organization which directs and unifies the work of all its branches.

Knowing the extent to which the work of this association is organ- ized all over the world as well as

In 1920, while the Mercury Herald touted the "splendidly equipped" building, the YWCA quietly bought the adjacent lot to expand.

Francisco and Los Angeles – these buildings remade San Jose. Public serv- ice agencies fed on the boom, too, with the construction of the Catholic Women's Center and expansion of the San Jose Day Nursery.

The YWCA kicked off a $125,000 annex campaign at a dinner at the Hotel Vendome on April 26, 1925. The drive looked and sounded much like the hoopla of 1914 – 10 days, an army of solicitors, a pitch to local pride and moral urgency. The campaign committee was a who's who of San Jose: The chairman was Paul L. Davies, a banker who would marry insecticide mag- nate John Crummey's daughter Faith, work at FMC and eventually rise to chairman and CEO. Members included John Crummey; developer T.S. Montgomery; William G. Alexander, a leading businessman and YMCA stalwart (and brother-in-law of Harriet Cory Hummel, who had returned to the Valley but not the YWCA); and Leonard P. Edwards, manager of the San Jose Abstract and Title Insurance Co., founded by his father. (Edwards would one day save the YW from financial collapse. His son Don would represent San Jose in Congress for 32 years, and his grandson Leonard would become a prominent Juvenile Court judge.) The indomitable Mesdames Beattie and Smith also served on the campaign committee.

The YW hired a campaign professional, Jean Rutherford. Women, of course, had proven their fund-raising mettle during the 1914 YW drive and World War I. But San Jose had apparently forgotten those lessons, judging by the reaction to Rutherford.

"When the city fathers and mothers saw her they threw up their hands in despair," a newspaper reported. "This pleasant young lady, with her blond bobbed hair, certainly could know little about finance, let alone trying to raise $125,000. Why, she didn't even look as if she could balance her own checkbook."

When the campaign closed, beating its goal with $128,098 in pledges, the paper declared, "She has done a so-called man's work, and done it well."

Some Second Street merchants objected to the expansion, and, for that matter, the very presence of the Blue Triangle. They called it "blight" on the commercial prospects for the block. They urged the association to sell and move, or at least line the street level of the building with shops. When the board politely refused, the merchants tried veiled threats: They reminded the board (and the architect, the contractor and men on the advisory council) that they donated generously to the Community Chest and sat on committees that judged the YW's requests for funding. The board and its supporters, however, held firm, convinced that the YWCA belonged in the city center. Downtown would change markedly decades later; leading institutions, including City Hall, the YMCA and the Mercury News, would move from the core. But the YWCA never abandoned its commitment to remain in the heart of San Jose.

Binder & Curtis, a San Jose architectural firm, designed the annex. (The board wanted to throw its business to local companies, but it probably did not hurt that this firm granted a price break. Ethically, the firm could not discount its fee so it charged full price – $8,656.35, or 6 percent of the building cost – and then donated $2,524.76 back to the YWCA.) The cornerstone was laid May 21, 1926. The building opened in December.

The four-story annex had 52 bedrooms. With the original wing reconfigured to add beds, the YWCA now accommodated 116 overnight guests — a significant increase, though far from the 250 beds the leaders initially hoped for. Fourteen beds were reserved for transients; most of the others were for "minimum wage" girls earning less than $100 a month. Each room had a lamp, desk, Windsor chair, bookshelves, rug and a touch of dainty flair: cream-colored walls, a porcelain sink and flower-print cretonne curtains with matching bedspreads.

The street-level cafeteria could serve 200 dinners a night and cater a banquet for 100. The board had high hopes for turning the eatery into a profit center. The kitchen boasted the latest electric amenities, including a blender and potato peeler.

Furnished and equipped, the building cost $175,754.11 — more, of course, than the board had planned or salted away in a bank. Nobody seemed alarmed, however. Emboldened by the success of the annex campaign, the directors voted to take a mortgage. They figured they could readily raise money to pay off the debt after 1928, when the final payments came due on the 1925 pledges.

On Jan. 18, 1927, the YWCA signed a 10-year $75,000 loan, at 6 percent annual interest, from Western States Life Insurance Co. of San Francisco. The association had to pay interest monthly and, in two years, start paying $5,000 annually toward the principal. The board had no trouble meeting the first principal payment, in January 1929. But nine months later, the stock market crashed, triggering the Great Depression. Instantly, donations collapsed and every public service agency that depended on them struggled to survive. The added burden of Loan No. 457 nearly crushed the YWCA.

CHAPTER
FOUR
1929 ~ 1940

Previous page: *Girls at Asilomar in 1933. The serene YWCA conference center hosted summer camps for Girl Reserves.*

CLASSES FOR THE MASSES

The Depression shattered the optimism of Santa Clara County and eroded its bounty. The fruit industry, the Valley's magnet and economic mainstay, saw prices and exports go into freefall. In *Silicon Valley, Women, and the California Dream*, historian Glenna Matthews notes that in hard times people still eat bread and potatoes – but they forgo prunes and canned peaches. The average weekly wage for Northern California cannery workers fell 50 percent from 1929 to 1933, to $8.04, according to Matthews. New home construction halted. The Community Chest failed to reach its fund-raising goals and reduced grants to agencies, including the YWCA.

For the first time since its resurrection in 1914, the association sank into the red. It borrowed cash from the Community Chest to pay taxes and insurance. The street-level cafeteria, envisioned as a source of income, operated at half-capacity and lost money. Like canned peaches, 25-cent pot roast, 10-cent mashed potatoes and even a nickel bowl of chocolate pudding suddenly represented luxuries beyond the means of many women.

The YWCA had one stroke of good fortune: Patricia Davidson as general secretary. Hired in 1926, Davidson had studied and traveled in Europe, and worked for YWCAs in Virginia, North Carolina and Santiago, Chile. She brought the stability and organization that had eluded the San Jose association and that would prove critical during a decade of financial turmoil. Everyone called her Miss Pat, the first general secretary to invite (or permit) such informality. Some board members found her warmth disconcerting, but the girls adored her.

Although the YWCA nationally still cleaved to Christianity, Bible-thumping programs were slipping from vogue. In 1920, the association eased its rules to allow any woman who signed on to its Christian purpose to become a member, not only women in evangelical churches. (The change opened the door to Roman Catholics, but the Vatican admonished them not to enter. As late as the 1960s, when the YWCA retained only the slimmest religious thread, influential clerics claimed the group promoted apostasy and spiritual indifference. The association did promote birth control and sex education, which probably did not win friends in Rome.)

By the early 1920s, National viewed itself as a crusader for causes that advanced the social implications of Christianity, which YW leaders defined as peace, justice and economic equity. During the Depression, these concerns naturally made the YW a champion of New Deal reforms (and almost as naturally, opened the group to false accusations of communism in the '50s). National advocated for the right to collective bargaining, legislation to improve wages and working conditions, and the creation of federal safety nets such as Social Security and unemployment insurance. National also promoted the expansion of services for women workers – and Davidson made this a priority in San Jose.

The YW had operated an employment bureau for years. At the October 1930 board meeting, Davidson proposed extending this to help women not only find jobs – hard enough in those years – but also figure out what work they would enjoy. Davidson described the "very new field" of vocational guidance and won board approval to offer it. She also recruited a volunteer to assist laid-off girls stranded miles from home without a dime for food or bus fare.

At the start of the Depression, the association had one club for business girls. By 1938, it sponsored seven clubs and a business league, with a total membership of 421. Stenographers, clerks, bookkeepers and department store workers belonged to the Argosy Club. Business-college students met mornings, as the Seven-Thirty Club, and evenings, as the Acme Club. Toastmistresses practiced speeches.

The Luncheon Club dished up food and short lectures on politics, history, literature and music. The very lively Tama-Thama Club (members claimed the name meant joy and laughter in Greek) held parties, picnics and trips with the YMCA. Girl Reserves who got jobs after high school joined GRAC, the Girl Reserves Alumni Club. Latinas met, briefly, as Contenta Hora. In 1939, the association organized a small club for domes-

A popular YWCA club for business girls, photographed in 1926, gave birth to seven clubs and the Business Girls' League by 1938.

tic workers and one for black women.

The YWCA had no club for workers in the canneries, a leading, though seasonal, employer of women. However, girls from the canneries formed basketball teams and competed in the YWCA gym before crowds as large as 250. The players even adopted a slogan: "Games for the masses, not the classes."

The Business Girls' League, formed in 1930, set up "interest groups" to encourage young women to mix across job (and class) lines. Groups ran the gamut – hula, ballet, watercolor, auto mechanics, exercise, sewing, flower arranging and work after marriage. If a few young women voiced interest in a topic, the YW helped them organize a group. Miss Pat, not an executive to hide behind her desk, led the debut session of a group on style and etiquette, "I Would Rather Be Right." She demonstrated how to walk with poise, enter a room with flair, sit and strike up conversation. For girls with a civics bent, "Know Your City" offered tours of the post office, the City Council chambers, a meatpacking plant and even the jail.

The YWCA, nationally and locally, envisioned clubs and groups as more than pleasant diversions. Davidson and her staff had three goals: to inspire women to continually learn – millinery today, the Gettysburg Address tomorrow; to break down class and racial divisions among women; and to mold leaders and fighters for social justice. Young women in San Jose participated heartily in the programs, but they did not exactly leap to the activist vanguard. This frustrated the staff and national evaluators who visited locals every three years to make sure they met YWCA standards.

In a 1936 report to National, Mildred Lowdon, director of business girls' activities in San Jose, complained that her members sought nothing nobler than friendships and fun. Although she said she had made them "more aware of the movements of working women and of the movements of peace," she had failed to rouse the girls to action. "They refuse to cooperate" with labor and peace organizations, she wrote. Lowdon did not fault the girls so much as their "farm town" environment, particularly the "rank conservatism" of the leaders and newspapers of San Jose.

Nevertheless, the progressive atmosphere of the Blue Triangle could only rub off on the girls. Though predominately white and Protestant, the residence, business groups and Girl Reserves included African-Americans, Latinas, Asians and Jews – a rare smattering of diversity in that era. In February 1937, the Business Girls' League hosted a YWCA regional conference and planned to house delegates in one downtown hotel. But it would not allow black delegates in the coffee shop, so the league switched to the Montgomery Hotel.

The business girls may not have jumped to the barricades for the big causes of the day, but they showed determination on an issue close to their hearts – smoking. They lobbied the board for years to allow them to light up in the building. In 1934, the directors finally relented. "The Y must keep up with trends of society in order to do the most good for girls and women," the board minutes said. "Since smoking has become fairly common in the better circles of society…it should not be prohibited and made shameful in the local building."

Compared with the business girls, the directors showed slightly more interest in the political and social upheavals of the 1930s. The board wrote to Congress calling for child labor laws, and to the state Legislature arguing against repeal of the minimum wage for women. (Members of YWCA business clubs throughout California kept detailed lists of their expenses, to demonstrate "the minimum on which a girl could decently live," according to the board minutes.) When the San Jose police chief called for the removal of immigrant children from public schools, the board advocated equal education for all.

Y.W.C.A Cafeteria

Entrees a la carte.

Fowl	.30	Breads & beverages.	.05
All roasts	.25	Extra pat of butter	.02
		Extra whipped cream	.03

Rolled lamb, all stews, ham cro-
quettes--New England boiled din-
ner--pickled or corned beef and
cabbage--fritters--kidneys,--
Stuffed beef heart--stiffed
peppers--breast of veal with
dressing--breast of lamb, short-
ribs--cube steak, chops, swiss
steak, flank steak--bacon and
apple ring--liver and bacon or
onions--tongue and spinach--
meat loaf--hamburger spanish--
bulk sausage and country gravy
chipped beef or tuna on toast--
all fish entrees, hash, meat-
pies, spanish rice, tamale pie,
goulash 20

Omelets, macaroni and cheese-
scrambled eggs or any entrees
which do not have meat as an
ingredient. 15

Vegetables

All vegetables (except the very
new in season, as new peas, corn
on cob) 05
    otherwise 10

Soups

Cup. 05
Bowl 10

Salads

Small salad. 05
Other salads . 10 .15 .20 .25

Cold plates consisting of a
Cold plates consisting of a cold
cut, potato chips, usually
potato salad--garnish. 25

****
Special   35¢

Includes choice of .15 or .20 entree
two vegetables (when entree is not
accompanied by rice, noodles, kraut,
cabbage, etc--then only one other
vegetable. Choice of 5¢ salad or 5¢
dessert , or 5¢ soup. Bread and
butter--roll or hot biscuits. Beverage.

****
Special   50¢

Choice of any entree except fowl
soup, salad, dessert, two vegetables
bread and butter, beverage.

****
Special   60¢

Chicken or turkey entree--otherwise
same as above.

****
Cloth napkin 2¢ extra

Dessert

Puddings, jello, ice cream, ice .05
Pie, cake, shortcake, tarts, cus-
tard, baked apple, fresh fruit
cobbler or any special dessert..10

Our cafeteria averaged not quite 300 meals per day during 1938

*The YWCA cafeteria served everything in 1938, even tongue with spinach.
A cloth napkin cost 2¢ extra.*

Still, unlike many YW leaders in large cities, San Jose's were politically cautious, and sometimes indifferent. At the urging of National, the San Jose YW established the Public Affairs Committee to promote study and action on issues such as consumer protection and unions. But the forums quickly died, for poor attendance. In many ways, San Jose *was* the farm town Lowdon had described, its conservatism steeled by hardship, its placid good-will lost amid vigilantism and violence.

In November 1933, a mob stormed the county jail and dragged out two men who had confessed to the kidnap and murder of Brooke Hart, the popular son of a department store owner and civic leader. One of the men was stripped naked; both were lynched and burned in St. James Park, as an estimated 5,000 to 10,000 people watched. In the early to mid-'30s, strikes in the fields and canneries ended in violence and arrests; during a 1931 strike of women cannery workers, police broke up a meeting with tear gas and fire hoses. The pillars of local power reviled the labor movement. These bankers, growers and canners were the husbands, fathers and dinner-party companions of YW directors, not to mention their staunchest advisers and donors.

YWCA ARCHIVES

A YWCA brochure underscored the focus on youth and international cooperation.

It was hardly surprising, then, that the board more comfortably embraced the international causes supported by National. World peace did not rankle a grower quite the way unions did. Fifteen San Jose women attended the 1937 regional meeting at Asilomar and they returned energized about the movement's global reach – more than 50 countries had YWCAs – and its pacifist bent. Mrs. Frederic Byl reported back to the board that women "everywhere were becoming peace-conscious," with the YWCA leading the way. It gave early, strong support to the League of Nations. And it was one of 11 women's organizations that organized the National Conference on the Cause and Cure of War in Washington, D.C. every January, beginning in 1925.

The national YWCA urged local associations to promote multicultural

The San Jose YWCA building saw its heyday in the 1930s and 1940s, as a hub for working women and a residence for San Jose State students.

understanding in their communities. No small task, given the insularity of most American cities. Nonetheless, San Jose took up that banner with vigor.

In November 1937, the YWCA held the All-Nations Dinner in Schofield Hall and asked every board member to invite a foreign-born guest. The event brought together immigrants from Mexico, Jamaica and Japan; second- and third-generation women from Germany and Sweden; and women who traced their ancestry to England and Scotland. Flags, songs, ethnic dances and food represented the various countries. The 1937 annual report called the dinner the year's "crowning achievement." The board decided to make it an annual event – and no wonder. In a bleak decade, with renewed rumbles of war in Europe, what could bring more joy than a celebration of solidarity among "peace-conscious" women, allied in a movement of tolerance, cooperation and a vision of a better world?

Another proud achievement was the success of the Girl Reserves. By 1938, the program had expanded to 21 schools and listed 427 members. In the YWCA spirit of developing leaders, each club elected officers and organized its own activities – picnics, parties, hikes and charity drives. (Self-determination, a worthy goal, turned out to be a mixed bag for teens unaccustomed to the expectation. Some clubs blossomed, but others foundered – another source of consternation for the YW staff.) The YWCA's Camp Ayun Mapu, at Big Basin near Boulder Creek, attracted about 150 girls for two-week sessions in the summer. More than 80 girls participated in the YWCA's Summer Fun in the downtown building.

Re-Elected President

Mrs. L. T. Smith, whose re-election as president of the Young Women's Christian association was announced at the annual meeting of the association last night.

MERCURY HERALD

YWCA doings made the news.

Through the 1930s, the YWCA board could look at its thriving programs and feel gratified. But the directors looked at the $75,000 debt with growing alarm. They made the first $5,000 principal payments on schedule, in 1929 and 1930. But they missed 1931. With every passing year, the association fell further behind and struggled more just to keep up with the monthly interest. The lender sometimes granted deferments, sometimes held firm and constantly sent threatening letters. One after another, board presidents – including Mrs. E.M. Jefferson, Mrs. Guy W. (Grace) Smith, and Mrs. Maude Empey – wrote, visited and pleaded for patience, or at least, better terms. In January 1937, when the loan came due, the YW still owed $56,000.

In 1936, '37 and '38, the board explored fund-raising options, from quiet overtures to loyal benefactors to a public campaign. But the directors either scrapped plans before starting because of the dismal economy, or they stopped soliciting midway because they had no hope of success. As foreclosure loomed, the board secretly discussed selling the building.

The YWCA silver anniversary banquet in Schofield Hall, on Jan. 19, 1940, offered no hint of the crisis. (At the time, the YW still claimed its birth as 1915, erasing its troubled early history. In 1955, when the international YWCA celebrated 100 years, San Jose moved its official founding back to 1905. Thus, its 50th anniversary conveniently coincided with the global centennial, but it came only five years after San Jose's 35th birthday party.) State Sen. Frank Benson, chair of the 1914 building campaign, cheerfully reminisced about the last-minute scramble to reach that goal, as if near-disasters were bygones. William G. Alexander, whose wife, Edith, had helped found, and fold, the original San Jose YW, slathered on the gloss: "With a great past behind you, the future must be bright."

The future, however, could not have looked darker. Two weeks after the dinner, the men's advisory council told the board to prepare to lose the building. The directors invited Jean Rutherford, organizer of the 1925 campaign, to an emergency meeting Feb. 7. She insisted that they could pull off a capital drive. Iva Smith, a board stalwart and chair of the finance committee, reported this to the men, who sharply disagreed. The directors voted to go ahead, in an unusual defiance of their powerful advisers. But Smith refused to lead the drive without them. Suddenly, the debt threatened to destroy something even more precious than the property: relationships forged in common purpose and built over years.

On Feb. 14, the board rescinded the vote approving the campaign. Smith drove to Sacramento to ask the loan officer for a moratorium on payment. He refused.

A few weeks later, the YWCA suffered another blow. Miss Pat resigned. Several directors cried at the announcement and again at her final board meeting, April 17. Davidson said she planned to travel and rest. The directors and staff presented her with two suitcases and a life membership to the YWCA in Santa Clara Valley. The gifts expressed more optimism than anyone likely felt. War was spreading across Europe and Asia, restricting travel. And nobody knew if the YWCA would survive the year, much less Miss Pat's lifetime.

CHAPTER
FIVE
1940 ~ 1949

WINDS OF CHANGE

As the country braced for yet another war, the YWCA tried to set aside its financial headaches and prepare, again, to serve the home front. Nobody yet knew that this war would alter the national landscape far more than the last war had – that thousands of women would go to work in shipyards and munitions plants; that Japanese Americans would be forced from their homes and interned in remote barbed-wire compounds; that blacks of the rural South would begin an unprecedented migration north and west. In early 1941, only one thing seemed clear. The military was growing rapidly. Soldiers and sailors were flooding into cities across America. And they needed what men in uniform always need: women.

At the request of President Franklin Delano Roosevelt, the YWCA joined with five other national organizations to coordinate spiritual, recreational and educational activities for the Armed Forces. USO, United Service Organizations, was incorporated in February 1941. That month, the San Jose YW organized a committee representing 15 women's groups to arrange dances for men at Moffett Field. The committee quickly announced a year's schedule and advertised for ladies "of the highest character," ages 18 to 25. To pass muster, a recruit had to submit letters testifying to her moral fitness.

Moffett authorities and San Jose officials applauded the committee's speedy action. But a Chamber of Commerce official wondered publicly how on earth the committee would round up enough suitable dance partners for all the Moffett air cadets. Not to worry. Hundreds of young women answered the call to serve. Students, nurses, bookkeepers, secretaries, teachers and shop clerks – everybody lusted to join the Victory Girls.

The committee held the first dance in March at Roosevelt Junior High

YWCA parties, such as this one in 1944, kept spirits up and stomachs full.

and 27 more that year. Downtown had a new Saturday evening ritual: young women dressed to the nines lining up in front of the YWCA. At 6:30 sharp, they flashed their orange VG cards, then dashed into the building or climbed into Army trucks that rumbled in convoys to Moffett.

At the height of the war, San Jose had 700 Victory Girls and dances every night. The girls ventured as far as Camp Roberts, near Paso Robles, leaving the YW on buses at noon, arriving for dinner, then fox-trotting till midnight. They slept on cots in the USO social hall. The dances were so much a part of wartime San Jose that the Mercury published each week's schedule. Dec. 6-12, 1943, was typical. Monday: Trinity Parish house, 60 girls. Tuesday: YWCA, 50 girls. Wednesday: Alexander Hall, YMCA, 50 girls. Thursday: Dance for College USO/VG, 75 girls. Friday: Catholic Women's Center, 60 girls. Saturday: Newman Hall, 60 girls. Saturday and Sunday: Camp Roberts and Fort Ord. Dancing, forbidden by the strict elders of the YWCA of World War I, now beckoned as a patriotic imperative.

There were other patriotic duties, of course. The Japanese bombing of Pearl Harbor roused fear throughout the nation, particularly on the West Coast. Within hours of the attack, a volunteer defense brigade posted watch at the railroad yards and industrial plants of Santa Clara County. Women from every organization, the YW included, marched door-to-door throughout the war, for government bonds, the Red Cross and the USO. The YW organized women to plant Victory Gardens, and fill boxes with plums and knitted socks to mail to soldiers overseas at Christmas. The association also trained high school girls, Valley Victory Volunteers, for jobs in the fields and canneries, with classes on how to pick and pack a tomato, how to prevent sunburn and how to strengthen leg muscles for standing from sunup until dusk.

Even the most mundane activities throbbed with flag-waving fervor. The YW no longer ran plain old exercise classes – it offered "Vitality for Victory:" calisthenics, badminton and volleyball to "ease war-weary minds." These Monday night sessions catered to employed women but they evidently weren't the only ones suffering wartime fatigue. The YW added "Fit for Defense," at 10:30 a.m. Wednesdays, for young matrons who did not work outside the home. It was the YW's first class geared to married women, who would become its main constituency in the 1950s.

While the demands of war reshaped the YWCA, the demands of the bank continued to haunt it. Months before Pearl Harbor, the association shut its money-losing cafeteria, sold the equipment and rented out the street-level space. (Tenants over the years included the Downtown Merchants Association, a beauty college and a salon.) The YW also closed the pool rather than make expensive repairs. The directors tried – and failed – to raise money to pay the debt. They had better luck refinancing the loan, a lifesaving breather. The new loan set monthly payments at a more or less manageable $405 and extended payments to 1951.

As the war dragged on, San Jose benefited from its happy byproduct – prosperity. The flush economy combined with rah-rah public spirit to increase donations to the Community Chest. In 1943, Leonard P. Edwards, a Chest leader and longtime member of the YWCA advisory council, organized a campaign to pay off the capital debt that threatened four local agencies: the YW, the Salvation Army, Volunteers of America and the Catholic Women's Center. Together, they owed $133,000.

Edwards insisted on a quiet appeal. No red tags or performing bicyclists, just letters, phone calls and face-to-face cajoling. It worked magnificently. On Jan. 1, 1944, the YWCA owed $50,530.05. A year later, it owed $23,741.81. By January 1946, all four agencies had erased their debts. They began planning a celebration.

On Feb. 25, 200 people came to a mortgage-burning party at the Elks

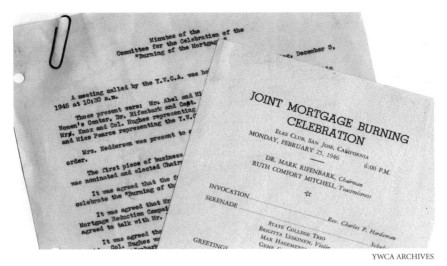

The YWCA celebrated the final payment on its mortgage by torching the loan documents. Two hundred people attended the party.

Club. Mrs. Christopher (Margaret) Nedderson, YW board president, torched the association's loan documents. A newspaper photograph captured the relief and euphoria of the moment. But the event left a bittersweet aftertaste. Maude Empey, a YWCA president in the late 1930s, summed up her feelings in a letter years later: "It's tragic, in a way, that it took a war to clear the building."

But the truth was, for all its pacifist leanings, war had always been a boon for the YWCA. The association got its start in England in 1855, helping nurses returning from the Crimean War. World War I catapulted the YWCA of the USA to national influence and brought new prestige to city associations like San Jose's. The demographic upheavals of World War II marked another turning point: They shaped an association that had always claimed to serve all women into a truly diverse movement and champion of civil rights. In 1946, 18 years before the passage of the U.S. Civil Rights Act, the national YWCA adopted an interracial charter. It declared the YWCA to be a "fellowship without barriers of race" and made an almost unimaginable commitment: "Wherever there is injustice on the basis of race, whether in the community, the nation, or the world, our protest must be clear and our labor for its removal vigorous and steady."

One of the greatest racial injustices in wartime America, of course, was the internment of Japanese Americans. In February 1942, President

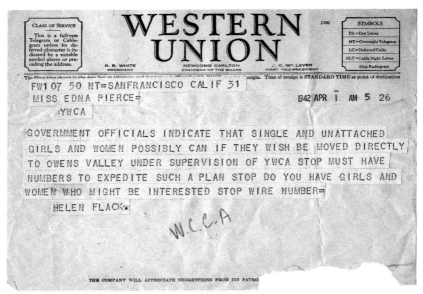

On the eve of the Japanese American evacuation, a telegram to the San Jose YW requested volunteers to supervise single women bound for an assembly center in Owens Valley.

Roosevelt signed Executive Order 9066, authorizing the evacuation of Japanese Americans from the West Coast. Beginning in May, the government moved approximately 120,000 men, women and children from their homes into assembly centers and then to 10 camps in isolated patches throughout the Western interior of the United States. The YWCA did not publicly protest – in the climate of war almost nobody did. But the YW spoke out against anti-Japanese bigotry. In a bulletin May 12, 1942, the eve of the evacuation, National told YW members in California, Oregon and Washington state that they had a "special responsibility" to support people being torn from their homes. "We have hundreds of Japanese American members. They are girls like us…they have worked with us in clubs, on committees and on boards of directors…they have helped build our coast economically and culturally." To those women, National made a promise: "Wherever you go, the YWCA will be there if at all possible."

The YWCA organized volunteers to accompany single Japanese American women on trains to assembly centers. Edna Pearce, general secretary in San Jose from 1940 to 1947, sent letters, newspaper clippings and YWCA announcements to women in the camps. It is impossible to know

HEART MOUNTAIN SENTINEL

Heart Mountain Sentinel, published at the Wyoming internment camp. Many Japanese Americans from San Jose were sent to Heart Mountain.

how many wrote back. An old YW binder has postcards from a woman named Chizuko Sameshima, addressed to Pearce from the Pomona Assembly Center and Heart Mountain in Wyoming.

Pearce also handled problems that may seem small in retrospect but reflect her sympathies. M. Itatani, a sergeant with a medical detachment at Camp Breckenridge, Ky., had left six cameras for safekeeping with the San Jose Police Department at the start of the war. (During the evacuation, Japanese Americans were forbidden to bring cameras.) In 1943, he asked a YWCA in Kentucky to help him get them back. The request reached Pearce on April 23. She appealed all the way to the U.S. Attorney in San Francisco to retrieve those cameras. Finally, on June 25, she packed them in a box to the sergeant, enclosing a note of good wishes and $3.10 because he had sent her too much postage.

The national YWCA dispatched staff to monitor conditions in internment camps and help women establish a branch wherever they wanted one. They wanted one in every camp. These YWs, run by women in the camps, offered standard association fare: sewing circles, business groups, Girl Reserves, all desperately needed diversions. More than that, the associations brought a measure of comfort to women stuck in distant, dusty prisons. The YWCA linked women to home and to a movement and assured them they had not been forgotten.

In a commemorative book published in 1994, Joy Takeyama Hashimoto of Salt Lake City recalled camp visits by national YWCA workers. "They understood the need for women and girls to continue to value their self-dignity and develop their potential abilities and leadership. This meant a great deal to the internees, and many continued to be active with the YWCA after their release."

YU-AI KAI

Portrait of Misao and Francis Hayashi and their sons taken May 5, 1942, when they were evacuated from their home. Misao Hayashi later joined the board of the San Jose YW.

Misao Hayashi, who had lived in Portland before the war, felt forever grateful to the YW volunteers who came to the assembly center where she, her husband, Francis, and their two sons slept in animal stalls. The YW women demanded that the dirt floors be covered with wood. The family settled in San Jose in 1953, when Francis Hayashi was appointed pastor of Wesley United Methodist Church in Japantown. Misao promptly volunteered for the YWCA. In 1955, she became the first Japanese American elected to the board. Later, Misao encouraged her daughter-in-law to get involved, and Helen Hayashi did, with fierce dedication. Helen joined the board in the 1970s, served as president in 1980-81 and led more committees over three decades than she could count. In 2005, she was still on the board, as first vice president. She, too, never forgot the women who fought to get a young family off a dirt floor. "The YWCA is a movement that works for justice and dignity," she said.

The Hi-Spot, opened in 1944, was a jumping joint for teens well into the 1950s.

One of the most successful San Jose YW initiatives in the 1940s had nothing to do with the war, though in its own way it had to do with justice. After years of jealously observing the Victory Girls, high school YW members decided they, too, wanted dances. They asked the staff to open a coed hangout. In October 1943, the board approved – though more from an impulse to protect the teens than provide equal access to parties. "With so many young men who were not old enough to be in the war hanging around First Street, and young girls becoming starry eyed over the uniformed guys in town, the idea quickly took hold," recalled Gloria Silva Jabaut, a president of the teen club.

The board allocated $50 to paint a small basement room and install stools and a snack bar. The center opened Feb. 26, 1944, directed by Ruthadele Taylor Sarter and later, Elsie Knobel Ryan. It was a hit overnight. Without asking for a dime, the center received $500 in donations and an anonymous gift of a jukebox. By March, the place drew 500 teens on an average Friday night and more than 100 after school. In April, the teens painted a second room to accommodate the crowds, and christened the place the Hi-Spot.

"The Hi-Spot was *the* place," Jabaut recalled. "Mrs. Ryan was like a second mother to many kids and certainly during that time with no school counselors, became one to lots of teens." Jabaut met her husband at the club – and theirs was not the only romance to bloom in the basement of the YWCA.

The Hi-Spot marked the YWCA's first independent coed venture. (It had sponsored a few coed activities with the YMCA.) "For a dollar a year, it was the best investment a boy or girl could make," Jabaut said. The club operated by the principles that governed every YW program. No mere hangout, the Hi-Spot encouraged leadership and self-determination. A teen council set rules and managed the budget. Teens planned the parties, cleaned up and collected dues. The Hi-Spot even had its own court. When a kid picked a fight or damaged property, a jury of peers convened to hear the story, pass judgment and set sentence. This ranged from several hours of hard labor (painting, scraping floors) to suspension.

The Hi-Spot celebrated its first birthday with 999 members and spreading renown. Youth professionals from around the state visited and took the idea back to their communities. Hi-Spot members took a leading role in a statewide youth council – Jabaut represented San Jose at the first Governor's youth conference, in Sacramento in 1950. Every Sunday, the Mercury published "Hi-Spot News," edited by the teens.

The column, of course, signaled the club's popularity but it also hinted at the changing face of the YWCA. Wartime had shaken up the Blue Triangle, that sober protector of young single women. First came the merry Victory Girls. Then badminton for matrons. Now, Sinatra records for soda-swilling teens. What was next? Classes for pregnant 16-year-olds? Clubs for retirees? Men on the YWCA board?

CHAPTER
SIX

1949 ~ 1970

FROM BAKE-OFFS TO BLACK POWER

T he years after the Second World War brought stunning changes to the United States, nowhere more than California and the Santa Clara Valley. Men who had passed through as soldiers returned with brides. People moved in from every part of the country, lured by jobs in defense and electronics. Vast stretches of orchards that burst into glorious flower every spring, the bountiful landscape known as the Valley of Heart's Delight, disappeared under freeways, tract homes, schools and industrial parks. The population of San Jose doubled in the 1950s, to 200,000, and more than doubled again in the 1960s. The city annexed surrounding communities like a conquering king, to grow from 17 square miles in 1950 to 68 square miles in 1960 to 136 square miles in 1970, a sprawl with 460,000 residents.

The YWCA spread right along with the city, carting its classes to neighborhoods and subdivisions. As Rosie the Riveter gave way to June Cleaver, the Blue Triangle focused less on working women and more on young wives at home. As the civil rights movement gained steam and the complexion of San Jose changed, the YW developed ethnic programs, hired Spanish-speaking staff and began to diversify a board that, for all the talk of tolerance, had been all white, all Christian for nearly half a century.

The YWCA, nationally and locally, had always claimed one of its greatest strengths was flexibility, as it nimbly changed to meet the needs of each new generation. But never before had the YWCA juggled such disparate needs and rapidly shifting demands. It responded with a mix of activities that is

Membership in YWCA clubs soared in the 1950s. Above: Y-Teens checked the progress of a recruitment drive in 1954.

almost impossible to fathom in a 21st century obsessed with niche marketing. In a single year, 1949, the San Jose YWCA organized a meeting on race relations, a fashion show with all the flounce of the postwar era, a delegation to a conference on international human rights and a course, "The Art of Being a Homemaker," with exuberant demonstrations of hat-making, low-budget cooking and sewing-machine attachments. That year, too, the YW launched Ladies' Day Out, to provide a break from the tedium and isolation of all that artful homemaking.

Ladies' Day Out would become the signature of the YWCA of the 1950s. It initially met Wednesdays from 10 a.m. to 2 p.m. in Schofield Hall. Classes, or "interest groups," were standard YW: sewing, rug braiding, copper enameling and flower arranging. A newspaper dubbed the ladies "hobby-happy matrons." But the main draw wasn't crafts. It was an innovation that later generations would call child care.

The YW called it a nursery with attendants. The association first offered it in 1947, so mothers could attend meetings of a new club, Y-Wives. At the time, few middle-class women would dream of leaving a 3-year-old with a paid stranger so she could work, let alone indulge in a few hours with friends. The idea remained unsettling, if not controversial, for years – at least in the popular mind. In 1958, when Ladies' Day Out started in Milpitas, a newspaper sought reassurance from no less an authority than Dr. Spock. The good pediatrician gave thumbs up: All classes accompanied by baby-sitting boosted the morale of mothers, he said, and that inevitably benefited their kids.

Many women, however, did not wait for the seal of approval. They flocked to Ladies' Day Out wherever the YW offered it. Just about every other YW program thrived, too – not since the early years of the YWCA had the people of San Jose shown such an appetite for clubs. Y-Teens, formerly Girl Reserves, formed groups in a dozen schools. Y-Wives met two evenings a month for classes, followed by coffee with the husbands. In 1954, Live Y'ers, for single men and women, began meeting Friday nights, and membership in the Hi-Spot peaked, at 2,544.

Only one club, Fille Amitie, languished. The descendant of the original YWCA clubs for business girls, Fille Amitie served employed young women. To drum up interest, Fille Amitie organized discussions on career development, lectures on politics and dances with servicemen. Only about a dozen women showed up. Finally, someone suggested reaching out to women who happened to work but planned to become housewives – women who saw career as interlude, not destiny. Fille Amitie announced a course, "The Art of Being a Woman," with classes on hair and clothing for business, preparation for marriage and adaptation to life in the kitchen. Weekly attendance jumped to more than 50.

Ruthadele Sarter, founder of the Hi-Spot and the YWCA-Cambrian Center

In 1951, women in Palo Alto established the Mid-Peninsula YWCA. A year later, the San Jose YW recognized the need to truck its programs to the suburbs because women would not venture downtown. In April 1956, the association launched Ladies' Day Out in a rented room at Cambrian Park United Methodist Church. Women came every Tuesday and called themselves the Cambrianettes. Two years later, Ladies' Day Out opened Wednesdays at the Milpitas Veterans Hall. The group named itself the Merry Wednesday Club. Ladies' Day Out met Thursdays at the Gloria Dei Lutheran Church in southeast San Jose, as the Edenettes.

From the '50s through the early '70s, almost all the growth of the YW

Junior high school girls found time to boogie at a Y-Teens conference in Sacramento in 1956.

took place in the suburbs. YWCA-Cambrian Center, the first full-fledged branch, opened at 4343 Leigh Ave. in April 1964 under Program Director Ruthadele Sarter. She had started the Hi-Spot 20 years earlier, the most popular YW club ever, and now she presided over the next giant hit. Only seven months after the Cambrian Center opened, Sarter pressed the board for more space and staff to keep up with demand. In 1965, the center recorded 394 adult members, 297 girls and 362 children spending time in the nursery. One hundred volunteers assisted with 66 classes and clubs, which recorded a total attendance of 8,750. Within 18 months of the center's opening, one-third of all YWCA activities took place at Cambrian. The committee that oversaw the center became a training ground for YW leaders for the next 20 years.

The YW established Eastside and South San Jose satellites and, in 1972, a Sunnyvale branch on South Murphy Avenue. Like Cambrian, Sunnyvale outgrew its space almost as soon it opened. In 1976, it moved to larger quarters across the street.

The YWCA outposts helped anchor new communities. Nurseries, sum-

Susanne Wilson and Lois Cullison at the national convention in Boston in 1967.

mer camps, classes and wives' clubs forged lifelong friendships and traditions. The Y-Zingers, a choral group at Cambrian in the 1970s, was still performing at churches and retirement homes 30 years later, long after leaving the YW and calling itself, simply, the Zingers. Volunteer Joleen Callahan's hiking group, formed at Cambrian in the mid-1970s, was still tramping the trails in 2005, the last vestige of adult programming at YWCA-West Valley, as the Cambrian Center would be renamed. Callahan herself still served on the YW board of directors. The West Valley child-care center, originally a nursery for women attending YW classes, also was going strong in 2005. Some of the staff had worked there more than 20 years and now cared for the kids of some of the first children to come through.

Many women at home raising families signed up for a lighthearted class or club at their neighborhood YW and got hooked. The association incubated talents, passions and ambition its members had never imagined. In 1962, Sarter recruited Susanne B. Wilson, her close friend from Cambrian Park Methodist, to teach sewing for the YW summer program there. Wilson had recently moved from Texas with her husband, Robert, an IBM engineer, and their three sons. Soon, Sarter prodded Wilson to join the board. "She

Cambrianette Marie Moore and Misao Hayashi, a longtime YWCA volunteer and director, in 1973.

saw things in me I hadn't recognized in myself," Wilson recalled years later in an interview with Mercury News columnist Leigh Weimers.

Wilson served as YWCA president from 1967 to 1970, explosive years for the association and a turning point for her. In 1973, at age 44, she ran for San Jose City Council. She didn't have lifelong old-boy ties but she had feisty Texas charm, and her YW years had taught her how to court power brokers, cut deals and raise money. Her friends at the YW and grassroots groups all over town walked precincts and stuffed envelopes to propel her into office. She served two terms on the council, becoming vice mayor. In her spare time, she earned a bachelor's degree in political science at San Jose State. She then spent 12 years on the Santa Clara County Board of Supervisors, rising to chairwoman.

If the YWCA gave Wilson her start, she more than repaid the favor. For years she watched over the YW like a guardian angel – adviser, cheerleader, strategist, negotiator, dreamer and fund-raiser supreme. In the mid-1980s, Wilson helped spark the YWCA's grandest venture yet: a new headquarters and residence downtown. Then she drove the multimillion-dollar campaign that turned a brash idea into an impressive building on South Third Street, with a residence that bore her name.

The Rev. Ralph Jackson, the Rev. Martin Luther King Jr. and the Rev. Ralph Abernathy during a civil rights march in Memphis in 1968. Racial justice became a hallmark of the YWCA.

But that was years later. In the mid-'50s and 1960s, when engineers' wives and PTA moms stumbled across the YWCA, America sat on the cusp of epic social change. Women like Wilson came of age in the day of June Cleaver, but they came into their own in the day of Angela Davis. Along the way, the national YWCA gelled into the movement it had long claimed to be – crusading for civil rights, racial justice and equity for women. Women in San Jose joined the march, tiptoeing at first, then stomping with gusto and eventually leading the way.

The first changes happened internally. The board slowly diversified. Misao Hayashi and Kei Ishikawa joined in the mid-1950s, the first Japanese Americans. In 1959, Evelyn Hammer became the first Jewish director. She went on to serve many years as treasurer. (Her son, Phil, a prominent attorney, later recalled her board tenure as one of her proudest achievements. Her daughter-in-law, Susan Hammer, San Jose mayor from 1991 to 1998, strongly supported the association both in and out of office.)

Lois M. Cullison, a social worker by training and a forceful YWCA administrator, arrived as executive secretary (the new name for general sec-

Closer to home, pickets from the Congress of Racial Equality protested at a meeting of the Christian Laymen's Association in Sunnyvale, 1964.

retary) in 1959. Whether it was her leadership, the times or a combination, Cullison nudged the board into the political currents coursing through America. The monthly board meetings, which had opened with prayer or biblical contemplation since before the Great Earthquake, now seized new inspiration: a reading from the Rev. Martin Luther King Jr., an update on the lunch-counter sit-ins in the South, a meditation on women's liberation, a discourse on urban renewal and the loneliness of contemporary life. Then, as always, the women moved on to board business. But that, too, took on new breadth and an edgier tone.

In 1961, the board voiced support for the black students conducting sit-ins in the South. The directors argued heatedly about their wording, to make it clear they endorsed only the goal of desegregation, not the televised protests. Most of the women frankly disapproved of noisy demonstrations – the YWCA board, after all, had rarely engaged in a political act louder than writing to Congress. But cautious as it was, the sit-in statement allied the YW with the emerging civil rights movement years before almost anyone else in San Jose took a public stand.

At an Asilomar conference in early 1963, Edith M. Lerrigo, head of the national YW, articulated ideas just beginning to swirl in San Jose. In a fiery speech, Lerrigo hammered the concept that the YW was a movement, not merely an organization. In these tumultuous times, amid growing racial strife, campus unrest and the first stirrings of the women's movement, YWs everywhere had a duty to lead the fight for equality and justice, she said.

Lerrigo looked at the women in the audience and issued a challenge: Whatever the cost, never sacrifice your beliefs to local sentiment. And do not content yourselves with quietly running worthy programs for girls.

The San Jose delegation listened, inspired. For some, it would not be an exaggeration to call the speech life-altering. Board President Lucille Wright returned to San Jose and instructed every club of the YWCA, every employee and director, to pledge at least one leadership action for 1963.

The March board meeting pulsed with the revivalist fervor of long ago. One by one, women testified. The Cambrianettes promised a year of study and self-scrutiny to learn about the YWCA as a movement and determine what role they would play. Cullison pledged to train the staff on the ethical underpinnings of YWCA programs. The board vowed to invigorate the Public Affairs Committee to take stands on such community issues as substandard housing and high-school dropout rates. The committee, lackluster for decades, suddenly leaped to center stage of the association – and far in front of community opinion.

In 1963, the YWCA supported the Rumford Act, which made California one of the first states to ban housing discrimination on the basis of race and national origin. Almost as soon as the law took effect, opponents got Proposition 14 on the ballot to repeal it. In February 1964, at the urging of the Public Affairs Committee, the YW board voted 11-3 to fight Prop. 14. The directors waged the battle with an earnestness that marked all YW endeavors, firm in the faith that through education, rational humans would see the light.

No placards or pickets for these women – they ordered every YWCA club to show a film on property values and race. They also held a week of meetings to stir opposition to the measure. (Only the Mid-Peninsula, Berkeley and Modoc County voted against Prop. 14, which passed statewide by a 2-1 margin. In 1967, the U.S. Supreme Court overturned the measure, restoring fair housing protections and vindicating the YWCA.)

The 1964 triennial national YWCA convention in Cleveland called for immediate integration of schools, housing, jobs and the association itself. The delegates voted to drop the pledge of Christian faith required for voting membership. Finally, Catholics, Jews, atheists – any woman who found the pledge difficult if not impossible to swallow – could readily join one of the oldest, largest women's organizations in the world as a full member. Under national rules, however, leaders still had to affirm their commitment to Christ (though in many locals, including San Jose's, directors had begun to look the other way).

At the 1967 convention, delegates voted to disaffiliate any local "not fully integrated in policy and practice." The YW also loosened its religious bindings even further. The association declared that while it remained "rooted in the Christian faith," its members and leaders did not have to be. The national association adopted a non-religious purpose: to "draw together women and girls of diverse experiences and faiths, that their lives may be open to new understanding and deeper relationships and that together they may join the struggle for peace and justice."

San Jose supported the 1964, and more controversial 1967, changes in membership rules. The board had debated the latter for two years before concluding what seemed obvious in hindsight: religious exclusions were no longer tenable, not for an organization hell-bent on equality and certainly not for one in a community growing more diverse by the day. As President Fern Topham wrote to National: "In the San Jose area, events of the postwar years have been so dramatic and so overwhelming that change has been inescapable. Our membership and program have been challenged to meet these changes in an atmosphere that is ethically Christian, but not evangelical. Our membership includes many who are Christian, but also many who are Jewish and Buddhist as well as those who have not expressed any commitment of faith."

Board member Yvonne Stanley

The board recruited members of color. Carmen Ponce and Rose Romero, the first Latinas, joined in 1970, followed a year later by Dolores Cedillo and Carmen Garcia. Yvonne Stanley and Betty Baldwin, and then Inez Jackson, were the first African-American board members.

The YW also brought new liberalism to its programs.

In August 1967, the YWCA and San Jose Unified School District began planning what was once unthinkable, and as yet forbidden: high school classes for pregnant teens. At the same time, the YW pushed for state legislation allowing pregnant students to continue schooling instead of forcing them to be tutored at home. Gov. Ronald Reagan signed the law that November. A few days later, Schofield Hall welcomed the Unwed Mothers Group, on Mondays, Wednesdays and Fridays. The group began with six young women and quickly grew to 11. By June it had 20 students, a waiting list and a new name, the Young Mothers Program, because some of the teens were, in fact, married.

Teachers from the school district handled academics from 9 a.m. to noon, and then YW women taught an hour of sewing and cooking. A public health nurse took the students on hospital maternity tours and counseled them on prenatal and baby care. Nobody judged the young women, or, even more remarkably for the times, told them whether or not to keep their babies. "The girl decides that," Virginia Michaels, a guidance coordinator for the school district, told a newspaper.

By the end of the 1960s, the San Jose YW embraced a broad political agenda. Along with National, San Jose supported gun registration, legalized abortion and sex education. Nationally and locally, however, the dominant issue was race.

Dorothy Height, national YWCA leader and civil rights activist

Like the civil rights movement, the YWCA was growing more militant. In 1969, National renamed its Office of Racial Integration. The new Office of Racial Justice, headed by Dorothy Height, adopted the language and aspirations of black empowerment. (An African-American leader who had worked with the Rev. Martin Luther King Jr. and advised presidents from Eisenhower to Clinton, Height spent 33 years at the national YW. More than any other person, she is credited with forcing it to live by the values it espoused. At age 12, she had been refused entrance to an all-white YW pool in Pittsburgh, Pa.)

The YWCA called for eight Racial Justice Institutes to be held around the country, where women of all races would identify ways to promote power and economic development in the African-American community. The Mid-Peninsula YWCA, in Palo Alto, hosted the first institute that September. Five San Jose women attended the three-day meeting, which turned into a referendum on black power within the YWCA.

Black delegates demanded support for an all-black national YW conference as a prelude to the 1970 triennial in Houston. Long, painful argument followed: Didn't blacks already have equal rights in the YWCA? Was the cause of racial justice uniting the association – or splitting it apart?

Finally, the institute unanimously endorsed the separate conference. Next, the delegates had to figure out how to pay for it. The national YWCA had no budget for such a meeting, and black delegates alone could not finance it. Would local associations – almost always strapped for funds –

'Y' dialogue helps ease racial tension

Women in this area are invited to join the Y's Dialogue Program, calling for meetings of small groups of those with diversified backgrounds to bridge the gaps of understanding during a time of national racial crisis.

All women are welcome to participate in the program sponsored by the San Jose Young Women's Christian Association, a United Fund Agency which serves the area from Milpitas west to Los Gatos and from South San Jose north to Sunnyvale. Those interested should call the San Jose YWCA, 292-5727.

These sessions are being organized at the suggestion of the national board of the YWCA. The format is local, outlined by a committee chaired by Mrs. William

they will meet informally, but with a loosely structured program outlines by the YW committee and with a moderator. There will be at least six sessions for each group, according to Mrs. Reeves, and they will be conducted in homes.

However, these will not be tea party sessions, the committee chairman declared. They will be designed to bring out differences so that a member can understand the feelings of other members. Groups will have constant reminders they are discussing ideas and attitudes, not personalities, and that each person has a right to be heard. As a technique for reminding participants that must come in the door with an objective view as possible, the

Important dialogue

They may be drinking coffee, but this isn't just an ordinary "cookie push" for Mrs. William Reeves (left), east San Jose; Mrs. Walter Svenson (center), Milpitas, and Mrs. Charles Stanley, Cambrian area. They're demonstrating how women will be coming together in groups to talk out their feelings on one of the most crucial problems of

MERCURY NEWS

The YWCA organized coffee klatches in living rooms throughout the Valley, where women and couples discussed their feelings about race.

share the cost? Susie Wilson stood and made the pledge that got the ball rolling: $100 from the San Jose board. Not until the board meeting six weeks later, however, did she request, and receive, approval for the contribution.

On April 10, 1970, 491 black women from 141 associations, including San Jose, gathered in Houston for the National Conference for Black Women in the YWCA. They denounced what they called the gap between association ideals and practices. The women demanded that the full convention adopt as the YWCA's "One Imperative" – its most urgent priority – the elimination of racism "by any means necessary."

The 25th YWCA National Convention met April 13-18. San Jose sent nine women, five of them as voting delegates: Baldwin, Mae Dailey, Jackie Howes, Sarter and Wilson. The One Imperative passed unanimously.

It was, without question, the most controversial step ever taken by the YWCA. Back in San Jose, some directors bristled, especially at that provocative phrase, by any means necessary. At the April 27 board meeting, the San Jose delegation tried to convey the rapture of Houston. With the One Imperative, Executive Secretary Lois Cullison told the board, "The YWCA made a covenant, like the Children of Israel," to go and struggle, full of faith, hope, determination, joy and the power of the Lord. "Go and struggle," Cullison exhorted. "Go and struggle!" Wilson read a statement by Edith

San Jose sent nine women to the historic 1970 national convention, five of them as voting delegates. Top row, left to right: Lois Cullison, Emma Chittick, M. Warning, Karen Kurtz. Front row: Mae Dailey, Jackie Howes, Betty Baldwin, Ruthadele Sarter, Susie Wilson.

Lerrigo, the national leader: "I lie awake nights worrying about the YWCA, because institutionally the YWCA is dead unless we are renewed, unless we can drop our old rigid patterns, unless we can be freed, unless we can use the power that is ours, unless we become action-oriented, unless we move!"

But would the YWCA survive if it moved too far, if it changed beyond anything San Jose could recognize, or accept? J. Kenneth Challen, a prominent Realtor and member of the YWCA advisory council, told Wilson the One Imperative was "the worst thing" the group could have concocted. "You know," he predicted, sadly, "the YWCA is dead in this community."

CHAPTER
SEVEN
1970 ~ 1989

JUST DO IT

Women in the Valley grabbed on to the One Imperative, body, mind and spirit. Racial consciousness spread to every nook of the Blue Triangle, from the Second Street boardroom to Cambrian clubrooms to preschool playgroups in the Almaden Valley and Sunnyvale. The Cambrian Center offered a course, "Ethnic Cultures and Contributions," for kindergartners through sixth-graders. The association set up youth programs at Meyer School and the Tierra Nuestra apartment complex in East San Jose – sports, games, homework help and "get to know your community" trips to places like Villa Montalvo. In keeping with the national mandate to promote minority economic development, the board's Racial Justice Committee, an offshoot of Public Affairs, compiled a directory of black-owned businesses in San Jose. The 12-page booklet, published in 1971, had 58 listings.

Although groundbreaking for San Jose, such activities were tame for the times. The Watts riots in 1965, the Newark riots in '67, the vicious clubbing of protesters outside the '68 Chicago Democratic Convention, the fatal shootings during student demonstrations at Kent State University – bloody confrontations over race, politics and the Vietnam War seemed to be tearing the very fabric of America. These truly were "days of rage," as the radical group Weatherman called its week of protests in Chicago in 1969. Young black militants demanded not integration but power, not sit-ins at Woolworth's but armed revolt. The Black Panther Party, based in Oakland, vowed to destroy white capitalism – so forget that black business directory. In the Marin County Courthouse, an attempt to free a black revolutionary prisoner, George Jackson, ended in a shootout that left four people dead,

The Y-Teens club at Washington School attracted a diverse membership in 1970.

one of them a judge. Against this backdrop, the YWCA's race activities did not provoke white outrage or fear. But that changed when the association took up the cause of Angela Davis, perhaps the most notorious black revolutionary of the day.

Davis, one of the FBI's "most wanted criminals," was arrested in October 1970 and charged with murder, kidnap and conspiracy in connection with the Marin shootings. President Richard Nixon went on television to congratulate the FBI for her capture, effectively condemning her. On Nov. 5, 1970, the national YWCA called for a fair, just trial for Davis – with the presumption of innocence until proven guilty. Susie Wilson joined YWCA women from throughout the Bay Area to develop plans to monitor the Davis trial.

Suddenly, the YWCA found itself braving its own days of rage. Letters poured in from furious members and donors: Good Christian ladies had no business with Davis, a criminal, a Black Panther and, worst of all, a registered communist. Racial justice was a noble pursuit but messing with the Davis case verged on evil. "The YWCA has gone overboard in its attitude toward racism," a longtime association leader in San Francisco fumed in a

Angela Davis arrived in court. YWCA observers monitored the trial in San Jose. An all-white jury acquitted Davis of murder and conspiracy charges in 1972.

letter to National. "I think that sinister forces are at work in our land trying to undermine all that is finest, and I am ashamed that our present Y leaders have fallen prey to so much false thinking."

When the Davis trial moved from Marin to San Jose, the fallout did, too.

Concerned about the flak, Wilson called for a board vote authorizing YW staff and volunteers to monitor the trial. The board gave its support, at some cost. Caroline Crummey, the wife of John Crummey, who had supported and advised the YWCA since 1914, quit the board, though she continued to donate money for the rest of her life.

An all-white jury acquitted Davis in 1972, and the rancor within the association subsided. But the hell-raising spirit only grew stronger.

The San Jose board elected its first African-American president, Inez Jackson, in 1973. Jackson, a mother of six and the city's first black postal clerk, had just finished four years as president of the local chapter of the National Association for the Advancement of Colored People, which she had helped establish. The YW, like its counterparts around the country, began attracting a new breed – angry feminists and idealistic professionals of various colors and class who cared not a whit about cross-stitching or wives' clubs. They wanted to use the clout of the YWCA to change the status quo.

Two young women, who had met at a YWCA dialogue on race, started a multicultural nursery at the YW South branch at Almaden Hills United Methodist Church. Instead of the typical preschool fodder – blond, blue-eyed dolls, This Old Man, graham crackers – 4-year-olds played with colorful folk toys, danced to African drums and Andean flutes, and snacked on maize and taro. The founders set up a second nursery at the Sunnyvale YW.

Sunnyvale also housed Women Together, a clearinghouse of information on all matters of interest to the Ms. generation, including jobs, divorce, education, consciousness-raising and do-it-yourself pelvic exams. All the branches established multicultural libraries and created programs so different from any in the past that the YW had to invent names for them: sex education "for mothers and others;" racial "dialogues" on themes like "honest confrontation toward constructive action;" and "worry clinics," where women spilled their troubles. These drop-in-clinics evolved into weekly rap groups. "Becoming a Whole Woman," at the South branch, drew 15 to 20 women Thursday nights to vent about female myths and expectations that led to feelings of helplessness, inferiority and depression. The downtown YW organized a group for women considering divorce, a judgment-free venue for soul-searching and practical advice in a day when marital breakup still bore heavy stigma. The group was the forerunner of a program for displaced homemakers, started in 1979. That, in turn, evolved into Women in Transition in the 1980s.

All these groups, classes and initiatives recast the image of the YWCA, which had grown musty with the years. Journalists voiced astonishment, as if their own sweet grandmothers had suddenly ripped off their aprons and marched to the barricades, demanding equal rights. In a full-page story about the San Jose YW, on April 15, 1973, the Mercury News proclaimed: "The staid old lady has changed." A March 1975 headline in Redbook wondered, "Can the YWCA Really Swing?"

YW leaders, nationally and locally, reassured the public that the association hadn't changed *that* much. It still offered camps, swimming, crafts and most of the wholesome, beloved pursuits of yesteryear. And the YWCA had always battled for human rights, equity and justice – interracial for decades, a labor champion during the Depression, a supporter of peace and international cooperation. "The YW historically has been involved in social action," Doris G. Harrod, the associate executive director in San Jose, told a reporter.

But without question, the local YWCA of the '70s *was* different. Physically, through branches, it had moved from the center of town to its cutting edges. It was also moving that way psychologically, emotionally, socially and politically. Back in 1963, Edith Lerrigo, head of the national YW, had pressed locals to lead, not follow, their communities. At last, her command came to bear in San Jose. The YWCA had always stood as a force for good. More than ever before, it now acted as a force for change.

The Rape Crisis Center endures as one of the most important programs born in that spirit. In January 1973, after a series of rapes locally, a group of San Jose State students asked the YWCA to help organize a response. The association hesitated. Like most people, the staff and directors assumed that rape was fairly rare and that the police and courts handled it adequately. But the YW soon realized it was mistaken.

In May 1973, the YW established a 24-hour rape crisis line, the first in Santa Clara County and only the second in California. An answering service routed calls to the homes of trained volunteers. They told women how to report attacks and get treatment, and they accompanied victims to hospital exams, police interviews and court (in the event the perpetrator was arrested and charged). In December 1974, a young mother named Jackye Read (now McClure) called the hotline. She said she had been gagged, blindfolded and raped at home by a late-night intruder, while her daughters slept in the next room. Her questions tumbled out – not just the pragmatic, where do I go, what do I do, but also deeper agonies: What should I tell my daughters? How will my husband react?

For all their kindness and sympathy, however, the hotline volunteers did

The YWCA established a 24-hour rape crisis hotline, (408) 287-3000, and raised public awareness about sexual violence.

not know. Nobody did. On complex issues surrounding rape, everyone stumbled in the dark.

McClure went on to volunteer for the crisis line, determined to shed light on sexual assault. Later, she helped organize a speakers' bureau. In 1979, she became the director of Rape Crisis and presided over a tremendous expansion of services. The staff and volunteers gave speeches on rape wherever people gathered – colleges, libraries, senior centers. The program collaborated with the police, district attorney and county hospital – to the ire of some go-it-alone feminists who saw this as tantamount to sleeping with the enemy, but to the eternal benefit of assault survivors in Santa Clara County. McClure was the first civilian invited to teach in the advanced training required for San Jose police. She pushed Valley Medical Center to set aside a room for rape victims and stop making them wait in the crowded emergency room. She and her staff and volunteers collected pants, sweatshirts and sneakers and hauled them by the carton to VMC, to end the humiliating practice of discharging victims in hospital gowns after police had confiscated their clothes for evidence.

By the mid-1980s, San Jose had emerged as a national model for its sensitive, comprehensive approach to rape. The YWCA by no means deserved sole credit but it played a significant role in every step.

Another major legacy of the 1970s was outreach to the Hispanic community. The YWCA had served Mexican-American teens for years – by design, through the Girl Reserves and Y-Teen clubs in schools downtown and in East San Jose, and by happenstance, at the wildly popular Hi-Spot in the YWCA basement. The Hi-Spot had opened in 1944 with mostly Anglo girls, but as the downtown population changed, so did the membership. By 1953, it was more than 50 percent Mexican-American. The single largest group was Catholic boys, not exactly the YWCA's target audience. By 1959, when the YW closed the Hi-Spot, the membership was 63 percent boys, 88 percent Catholic and 83 percent Spanish speakers.

The shutdown made a certain sense for an association constantly struggling for money and always juggling to best serve its main constituency, girls and young women. But the end of a low-cost, centrally located, supervised teen club dealt a blow to kids who had little money and nowhere else to go.

"I have heard many regrets that the Hi-Spot has closed, and also wishes for it to reopen," Ruth Johansen, a teacher at Mayfair School in East San Jose, wrote to the YWCA in February 1960. "These young people have limited funds to spend and also feel rejected – here they found good companionship and a welcome reception and also had something they had built together."

The YW reopened the Hi-Spot, under pressure, a few months later. That step earned the association a civic award in 1961 for service to Mexican-Americans. But by the 1970s, the Hi-Spot was gone, along with the rest of the building (razed for redevelopment in 1973), and the association had little credibility in the Spanish-speaking community.

In 1976, a YWCA outreach worker contacted 20 Hispanic agencies to

A poster display at Eastridge mall in 1970 promoted the YWCA's commitment to multiculturalism and women's rights.

discuss joint efforts to serve women and teens. Three refused to meet with her. The others expressed skepticism, if not hostility, toward an association they perceived as white and middle-class. At the board meeting April 26, the directors heard the worker's report and created a task force on the needs of Spanish-speaking women. The directors also declared that they would strive to make the board and all YW committees racially representative of the San Jose region.

The Hispanic Program got off the ground in 1978. In 1980, it served more than 900 people, from 2-year-olds in Tiny Tots to retirees who played Mexican bingo in the mornings and U.S. bingo in the afternoons at Club Esperanza. Although the Hispanic Program offered YWCA classics like games and sports, it took the association into new territory, with classes in citizenship and English as a Second Language. In 1982, the YW renamed it the Multicultural Outreach Program.

Decades later, YW women recalled the association of the '70s as a kind of magical enterprise where anything seemed possible. No doubt, nostalgia had softened the frustrations – the ever-gnawing money troubles, the long years it took to build trust among Hispanics, the Kafkaesque tussles with the city Redevelopment Agency over the fate of the Second Street building. Still, the YW had the vigor and guts to try almost anything, a zest to just do it long before Nike emblazoned the slogan on T-shirts. The association supported, sponsored and sheltered many disparate groups simply because nobody else would. Rape Crisis, Club Esperanza and Women Together made headlines, but even groups that got little public notice made a big difference in people's lives: art groups, play groups, support groups for widows and divorcees; the Zingers and Joleen Callahan's walkers; African dance, sewing and self-defense classes on the Eastside.

"We had a lot of tenacity," McClure said. "We put our feet out there. When other people would say, 'Let's think about it, talk about it,' we didn't. We didn't have time to talk. We just went out there and did it."

In the 1980s, the association moved toward greater professionalism. Guided less by impulse and more by planning, the YWCA gradually lost much grassroots verve. But it gained influence, stability and grant money. The shift, naturally, began at the top. The board of directors, overwhelmingly churchwomen and matrons for more than three-quarters of a century, began to recruit professionals and business owners. More women earned their stripes, and paychecks, in the working world, and the YW scooped the cream of the growing crop. The 1982 board, the first with a majority of professionals, included Gail Fullerton, president of San Jose State, and Ruth Tunstall-Grant, a well-known artist and educator.

Soon the roster would list every profession, and many names notable not for their husbands' achievements but their own: policy aide (and later San Jose City Councilmember) Cindy Chavez; policy analyst (and later County Executive) Sally Reed; bankers Patricia Lowell and Pamela Bogle; stockbrokers Teresa Jones and Laurie Besteman, who launched the highly successful YWCA Professional Women's Luncheon; corporate executives Patsy Kimball and Julia Gillman; nonprofit executives Mary Ellen Heising and Susan Hayes; attorneys Janice Fox, Mary Katherine Kelley, Sandra Kloster and Michele McInaney; accountant Isabel Chiu; fund-raiser Caroline Punches; organizational psychologist Carrie Miles; pastor Glenda Thomas; physician Suzanne Austin; marketing and public relations pros Janet Dietz and Kay Mascoli; and high-tech manager Jenifer Williams, whose mother, Iola, served as San Jose's first black vice mayor and who would rise to YWCA president. The list of names went on and on and on.

The increasingly high-powered board began to view the YWCA through a business lens. Directors believed that to survive, the association had to move beyond worthy money-losers and develop "income-generating" ventures. Sure, these had to mesh with the YWCA's mission and values. But the board eyed the bottom line and pushed for growth.

Such calculations led the YW to create That's Women's Work, in 1983. It offered training in non-traditional jobs such as appliance repair and industrial cleaning. A year later, the association opened its first full-time child-care center – eventually, it would operate a dozen, then cut back in the recession of 2001-2004. Also in 1984, the YW significantly expanded its Career Center. (Eventually renamed the Employment Center, it, too, would fall victim to the recession 20 years later.)

The new initiatives earned A-plus reputations, but they had mixed success as businesses. The association insisted on keeping all programs affordable and well-staffed, which meant low fees and high costs – not a diet for a cash cow. Nevertheless, the board got the growth it wanted, almost dizzying growth in the mid-1980s, fed largely by grants and government contracts.

In 1983, the YW received its largest grant until then, $43,000 from the state to teach elementary school children how to recognize and report sexual attacks. (California was the first state to require such instruction, and the idea did not go over easy. A major corporate foundation in Silicon Valley refused to support the YWCA Child Abuse Prevention Program, CAPP, on the grounds that such lessons didn't belong in schools.) In 1985, the association received four grants totaling $500,000 – equal to the entire YWCA budget just a few years before – to expand CAPP, train teachers and develop materials in Spanish.

From 1983 to 1985, the YW staff more than quadrupled, from 14 to 60, not including instructors working on contract. Executive Director Faith Rein (the top job had been renamed again) and President Sarah Janigian launched two annual events that heaped public attention on the association: the Y-Walk downtown in 1984, in which volunteers enlisted sponsors to raise money for YWCA programs; and TWIN, Tribute to Women and Industry, in 1985. Based on a national YWCA recognition program, TWIN honored women in business and the professions, and their employers. Prestigious for the winners, TWIN proved infinitely valuable for a YWCA trying to reach out to corporate Silicon Valley.

The association also received its own hard-earned recognition in 1985. San Jose hosted the YWCA 30th National Convention, March 21-25. More than 1,200 delegates passed resolutions calling for pregnancy-prevention programs, full employment, equal pay for equal work and top-notch, affordable child care – a platform that would guide the association for years to come.

As 1985 drew to a close, Rein and the board developed a five-year plan for continued expansion and greater visibility. The strategy made sense: For all its changes, the YW had not grown nearly as dramatically as the community around it. Born in a dusty frontier town, raised in a conservative farming hub, the YWCA now stood at the heart of a sophisticated, liberal, affluent metropolis known around the globe as Silicon Valley. Innovation and hard-charging ambition seemed to permeate the air, and everyone breathed it – the women of the YW included. They hatched a creative, audacious plan for their future. In 1989, they unveiled it. The YWCA would build a five-story $14 million headquarters and housing project, unlike anything San Jose had ever seen.

CHAPTER
EIGHT
1989 ~ 1993

BIRTH OF A VILLAGE

The women envisioned not a building so much as a community of compassion. The YW would occupy the two lower floors. Low-income adults and single-parent families would live upstairs for as long as two years, while they set their lives on course. The YWCA would help them identify goals, manage budgets, go back to school, receive job training and find work. The association would also provide child care, health education, parent education and even a fitness center.

The YW called the project Villa Nueva, new village. The meld of apartments, offices and social services under one roof was unprecedented in San Jose, a low-rise sprawl of houses and strip malls. Villa Nueva sparked huge excitement in a city longing to see downtown rebound, and enormous pride in the association. "This is something economists and social scientists have said should be done," Susie Wilson told the Mercury News in March 1990. "And we're the first ones to do it."

YW women had dreamed of a new home for decades. The Second Street building had seen its heyday in the '30s and '40s, as a lively clubhouse, noisy dance hall, and women's hub when downtown still served as the nucleus of the city. San Jose State students filled the residence, giving it the carefree air of a sorority. A group that shared the third floor in the fall of 1944 – students from Redwood City, Fortuna, Bakersfield, Weed, Whittier, Mt. Shasta and Hawaii; girls who nicknamed one another Baby, Star, Popcorn, Playmate, La, Piggybanks, Bibs, Gart and Tiny – remained friends the rest of their lives. Sixty years later, members Stella Barreto-Cuffe, Nell Lambert Jacobson and Edith Hazell Barreto (Edith married Stella's brother the day after graduation) still relished the memories of life at the YWCA. They

The reception desk of the old YWCA building, at 210 S. Second St. The building was razed for redevelopment in 1973.

recounted them in a letter: the house matrons who "became our mothers away from home;" birthdays celebrated with a gardenia corsage and a group dinner at Bohannon's; the ring of an upstairs phone announcing a male visitor in the lobby; the constant singing. Once, as they sat down for supper at 5:30 p.m., a few of the girls conspired to jazz up grace, "much to the exasperation of one of our friends, a devout daughter of a Methodist minister. It took several days before she realized we were not being entirely sacrilegious. We just wanted to put a little lightheartedness into our prayer."

The luster of downtown began to fade in the 1950s, and the YWCA building was deteriorating. A 1957 YW report urged the board to decide whether to renovate or rebuild. In 1961, city officials seemed to settle the question when they tagged the YWCA for bulldozing as part of San Antonio Plaza Urban Renewal.

But then, nothing happened. The city crawled on San Antonio, leaving the association in an awkward limbo. Should the YW fix a building slated for demolition? Nobody knew when that might happen. Meanwhile, young women lived in increasingly shabby, if not unsafe, rooms. Should the board

*San Jose State students who lived at the YWCA in 1947 loved a good party,
like this Hawaiian bash. Men were not allowed in the residence.*

sell the building and leave the city core? The YMCA, the newspaper and
City Hall would take that route in the late '60s. It seemed logical for the
YWCA, too. But it felt wrong. The board believed firmly that the YWCA
needed a central location, near bus lines, to fulfill its mission to serve all
women in need.

In 1962, the YW completed a $25,000 makeover, a compromise between
a renovation and a move. New furniture and a black-and-white checker-
board vinyl floor spruced up the lobby. Pastel paint, rugs and linens fresh-
ened up the bedrooms. The front door was painted bright blue to match the
Blue Triangle. It was a temporary fix, and in 1965, with the city still dragging
on San Antonio, the board decided to knock down the old headquarters and
build again on the old lot on Second and San Antonio. But the city urged the
YWCA to hold off: San Antonio Plaza would break ground by 1967.

By early 1968, the plaza remained stalled. But the YW had identified a
promising site a block south of the original building, and hired local archi-
tects Steinberg and Associates to sketch plans. Everyone at the YWCA grew
excited about a move – and then the Redevelopment Agency complicated
the works. The agency said it would buy, condemn and demolish only the

north wing, the Julia Morgan portion opened in 1916. The YWCA could keep the south wing, the 1926 annex.

The directors were aghast. What would they do with half a building? Use it? Impossible. Sell it? Not likely. The women demanded that the city buy the whole place. Then they waited, again. The YWCA advisory panel minutes of April 2, 1968, reflected the mounting frustration. "We are at a standstill until the city decides, which may not be some years," the recording secretary lamented.

Meanwhile, the old building brought fresh headaches. Just weeks after the Redevelopment Agency offer, a new residence manager at the YW asked the Fire Department to advise her on evacuation procedures. Inspectors turned up 12 discrepancies from code. Fire officials ordered Schofield Hall closed to large groups until the YW installed automatic sprinklers and enclosed the stairways, at a cost of about $5,000.

The association did not have money to spend on a building on the redevelopment deathwatch. So the YWCA shut Schofield Hall, a gathering spot for women for more than half a century.

In April 1970, the YWCA bought two adjacent parcels – 36,500 square feet – bounded by Second and Third streets, between San Carlos and San Salvador streets. The lot cost $196,800. Architect Goodwin Steinberg drew ambitious plans for a two-story administrative building with a six-story women's residence behind. The association geared up for a major capital drive. As honorary chair, the YW selected Paul L. Davies, who had chaired the 1925 campaign.

But the board quickly recognized it had no hope of raising enough money, given the poor economy and high interest rates at the time. Moreover, the women realized that the plans reflected an outdated vision of the YWCA as a haven for single women. In the early 1970s, the residence languished at 60 percent occupancy. Downtown blight and the building's deterioration contributed to the falloff – narrow hallways, creaky floors, grimy windows and prostitutes on the corner made the place utterly dispiriting. But the problems ran deeper. San Jose State students rarely rented rooms anymore, preferring campus dorms or apartments. Most of the women living at the YWCA attended business and beauty schools. The residence had lifted its age limit of 35 to attract more working women, but they, too, wanted to live on their own, not in small bedrooms with no cooking, under a matron's watchful eye. The association surveyed YWCAs around California; most said they would not build a residence again.

The Villa Nueva complex, on the drawing board for four years, brought badly

The board shelved its plans for the site, and waited, yet again, for the city to clear the ground for San Antonio Plaza. In the spring of 1972, the Redevelopment Agency finally offered $453,790 for the north wing. The board held firm for $500,000, which would include the entire place. After a year of negotiations and court battle, the city bought the whole building for $500,000 and sent the YWCA an eviction notice.

The building at 210 S. Second St. closed May 31, 1973. Lois Cullison, the YW's top administrator, removed the cornerstones of 1915 and 1926, and gave plaques of appreciation to the employees, some of whom were losing their jobs. Before the wrecking crew arrived in October, Wilson persuaded a developer to dismantle Schofield Hall, redwood beam by beam, in hopes of preserving a chunk of history in a city not known for honoring its past. A young architect, Richard Zlatunich, donated his time to number every beam, so the hall could be re-assembled. Wilson imagined a recreated Schofield Hall at the new San Jose Historical Museum (now History San

needed low-income housing to San Jose.

Jose). The city agreed to store the redwood. But when YW women tracked it down more than a decade later, they discovered it had not been properly sheltered and had rotted.

The YWCA rented offices at 1066 W. Hedding St. and broke ground for a modest single-story headquarters. The building, at 375 S. Third St., opened in 1975, a scaled-down version of the administrative portion of the complex Steinberg had sketched in the 1960s. It contained a lobby with sofas, a small room for day care, a large activity room for exercise classes, a boardroom, a kitchen and several offices.

The building was conceived as the administrative center of a YWCA whose programs operated mainly in suburban satellites. But by the time the YW moved in, branch programs were waning. Women had less spare time, and many more options, for YW-style classes and clubs. Community colleges, city parks departments, fitness centers – suddenly everyone offered the sort of athletic, educational, recreational and self-help programs that

The Villa Nueva Building Committee, chaired by Mary Katherine Kelley, ate, breathed and slept the details of design and construction. Left to right: members Pamela Bogle, Faith Rein, Joleen Callahan, Kelley and Sarah Janigian.

the YW had pioneered or promoted. For its part, the association was moving away from sponsoring a huge assortment of classes and clubs led by volunteers, toward providing serious social services from a downtown agency supervised by professionals.

As the association bulked up on grants and staff in the mid-1980s, the building seemed close to bursting. The YW converted the child-care room, the boardroom and even the lobby into offices, with wall-to-wall desks. The directors drafted ambitious plans for expansion. But everyone knew the YWCA could not grow without a new building.

President Sarah Janigian and Executive Director Faith Rein began talking about the YWCA of their dreams. They brought in Mary Katherine Kelley, a board member and attorney, and Wilson, then a county supervisor. The group imagined a downtown headquarters that would stand as a monument to the vision of San Jose, just as the Julia Morgan building had when it opened. They believed the YW home must provide shelter – not the bedrooms of yesteryear, but housing geared to women and children of the late 20th century and beyond.

"In the recession of the early '80s, the Y would get tons of calls starting at 3:30 or 4:00 in the afternoon, from people looking for a place to sleep,"

Kelley later recalled. "Particularly women – they knew the Y had provided a place to stay in the past. It made us aware of the lack of facilities for these people. And it really bothered us."

Janigian, Kelley, Rein and Wilson became the driving force in a mammoth undertaking. It would test the YWCA and elevate its stature as never before. The association had always operated fairly unobtrusively and largely on its own. Now, it would forge highly publicized deals with powerful partners, Bridge Housing Corp., a San Francisco-based non-profit developer, and the San Jose Redevelopment Agency. The YW had always struggled financially. Now, it would spearhead a $14 million project financed by a complicated mix of grants and loans from the city, federally supported tax credits, bank loans and donations. The association had never run a fundraising campaign for more than $125,000. Now, the YWCA would have to come up with $2.5 million for its portion of Villa Nueva.

Rein had overseen construction of the YWCA in Toledo, Ohio, where she previously worked. But neither Janigian nor Kelley had building experience, unless you counted the fact that Kelley's dad used to work in the lumber business. As a Mercury News editorial later put it: "The board had to think big, ignore naysayers and know where to go for help."

Janigian, who served 16 years on the YW board, worked with Rein to oversee the project. Kelley chaired the building committee, managing deals, contracts and details of design and construction. Wilson and Jack Conner, chairman of Plaza Bank of Commerce in San Jose, chaired the campaign steering committee – the fund-raisers. The honorary chairs were Caroline Crummey and Faith Davies; stepmother and stepdaughter, best friends, the philanthropic divas of San Jose and widows of the men who had led the 1925 YWCA building drive. Scores of volunteers from the board and the community pitched in. The Steinberg Group designed the building, and developer Charles Davidson's firm L & D Construction built it.

By 1991, the YWCA had $3 million in pledges. Rein and her staff moved into rented offices at 440 N. First St., and the one-story administrative building came down. On May 22, at 11 a.m., Villa Nueva broke ground.

Construction proceeded steadily, with no more than the usual delays. But for the YW women who lived, breathed, talked and slept Villa Nueva, the next two years felt like an exhilarating, exhausting ride. At one point, the sewage backed up. Their well-liked contact at Bridge Housing was transferred and replaced. The wife of the construction manager was killed riding a bicycle, and YW women, as was their wont, surrounded him and his fam-

After breaking ground in May 1991, Villa Nueva construction proceeded steadily.

YWCA women donned hard hats to check out the view from the top.

Susie Wilson posed for a photograph for the Villa Nueva publicity blitz.

Villa Nueva enlivened a once-moribund stretch of Second and Third streets.

Youngsters from YWCA child-care centers made drawings of Villa Nueva after it opened. The illustrations were framed as thank-you gifts for donors.

ily with comfort and support. A major donor went bankrupt, reneging on one of the largest pledges. Rein resigned 10 months before the doors opened.

But for every heart-stopping setback, there were moments that seemed miraculous – a big donation landing out of nowhere or a difficult-to-negotiate loan suddenly sailing through. "It was one of those projects I think God was guiding," Kelley said. "There were so many times when we thought. 'Oh, we can't do this. We don't have the money.' Then something would happen and it would work out."

The thorniest issue turned out to be the dream itself. The notion of an urban refuge for women trying to turn their lives around embodied long-standing association ideals, but it conflicted with modern anti-discrimination laws – the very laws that the YWCA had boldly championed since the

1960s. Villa Nueva had to welcome all comers who fit the income qualifications: men as well as women, two-parent families as well as single moms, and the elderly as well as people just starting out. Moreover, the federal tax credit program that helped finance the project precluded transitional housing. The YW could, of course, help tenants get training, jobs and all the other resources that might lead them to bigger homes in settled neighborhoods. And the small apartments would naturally encourage turnover, especially as families grew. But Villa Nueva could not impose a time limit on residency. Tenants would have every right to stay as long as they liked.

As the building neared completion, YW women worked feverishly to raise money to pay construction loans. Janigian served boxed lunches to prospective donors, right there in the shell of the building. The women wrestled with scores of details, from the pros and cons of anti-graffiti paint, to child-safe spacing on window bars, to the ideal slope of the parking ramp, to the question of how to pay for furnishings – an obvious, though unbudgeted, need. The American Society of Interior Designers in Santa Clara County and Design Response, a non-profit interior design group in Campbell, swooped to the rescue. The groups recruited designers to decorate the rooms pro bono, and then rounded up donations of new furniture.

Villa Nueva opened to publicity, praise and a round of parties March 22-27, 1993. The 124,000-square-foot building, painted pinkish earth tones, had warmth, an almost feminine grace missing in the hulking edifices of the redeveloped downtown. Yet Villa Nueva had unmistakable presence. It ran from Third Street to Second Street, dominating the block between San Carlos and San Salvador. It had stately entrances, airy plazas, curved balconies, a tiled roof and gracious railings and chandeliers – a blend of modern and Spanish influences, with echoes of Julia Morgan's careful craftsmanship. The building contained YW offices, a child-care center and 63 apartments, including studios, one-bedroom and two-bedrooms, each with a small terrace. "Everything we hoped for was in place," Janigian said.

Alan Hess, architecture critic of the Mercury News, called Villa Nueva a model for urban living and a jewel for downtown. "This is a building that belongs to the city," he wrote. Henry Cisneros, then secretary of the U.S. Department of Housing and Urban Development, visited. But Villa Nueva gave the YWCA more than laurels for architecture and city planning. The building marked a triumph of the spirit, and a measure of the muscle, of an association approaching its centennial. "Instead of becoming dated and irrelevant, it has grown and changed to meet the needs of women and the

Children frolic in the playground of the Villa Nueva child-care center.

community," a Mercury News editorial said.

The first day Villa Nueva's Susanne B. Wilson Residence accepted applications, 600 poured in. Twelve hundred more arrived by the deadline two weeks later. The YW women who had devoted years to the project watched with the awe, the soul-stirring joy, of a mother cradling her newborn. "I used to tell people," Kelley later said, "that pink stucco was my life's blood."

Among YWCAs nationally, only San Jose cut the ribbon on a new building in 1993. Far more teetered or toppled altogether. That trend would accelerate over the next decade, bringing the most sweeping changes in a century to the national YWCA and forcing tough decisions in San Jose.

CHAPTER
NINE
1993 ~ 2005

DEFIANCE AND DEDICATION

With a grand new home in a flourishing downtown, the YWCA looked forward to growth, greater influence and, at last, stability. But as the millennium and then the YWCA centennial approached, the association rode a roller coaster of change. Boom and bust in Silicon Valley, turmoil in the national association, the collapse of YWCAs across the country – the San Jose YW had known ups and downs but never before did it whip so precipitously from perilous low to gratifying high.

The 1990s established the YW as one of the most potent, trusted agencies in the Valley. Judges from the juvenile and family courts, social workers, school principals and large employers turned to the association for help dealing with problems that, for all the glittering wealth of Silicon Valley (and sometimes because of that wealth), seemed to grow more urgent by the year: teen pregnancy, truancy and juvenile drug abuse, the trauma of divorce for children, the shortage of affordable child care for low-wage families. The YW launched and expanded programs at dizzying speed. And its budget soared, from $1.5 million in 1989 to $2.5 million in 1993 to $5.4 million in 2001.

The financial vigor heralded a new era for the association and women in general, who had usually tiptoed at the economic margins. It had taken the YW more than 80 years just to reach a $1 million budget. Seemingly overnight, it emerged as a powerhouse amid a rapidly expanding circle of successful women. To celebrate and capitalize on that circle, the YWCA launched the annual Professional Women's Luncheon at the Fairmont

Hotel in September 1991. Featuring playwright Wendy Wasserstein, that event drew more than 900 people and netted $82,000.

The audience could not help but marvel at itself: well-heeled women packing a ballroom and snapping open checkbooks to support work they admired. (The YW suggested a minimum donation of $100.) Years later – after contributing to dozens of deserving causes and lunching on a lifetime's worth of chicken salad nestled in endive – many women still recalled that first YW bash with astonishment, even misty eyes. "I remember walking into that room, and feeling amazed," said Jill Arnone, YW president from 1999 to 2001. "Wow! Here were all these intelligent women who could afford a hundred-dollar ticket, which was a lot of money back then."

The luncheon grew and in 1994, it moved to the San Jose McEnery Convention Center. Speakers included journalists Ellen Goodman, Anna Quindlen and Linda Ellerbee; astronauts Mae Jemison and Sally Ride; novelist Isabel Allende; actress and author Patty Duke. The audience gave standing ovations to Benazir Bhutto, former prime minister of Pakistan; Janet Reno, former United States attorney general; and the controversial Joycelyn Elders, who had been forced to resign as surgeon general after declaring that masturbation was part of human sexuality and perhaps should be acknowledged. The celebrity speakers brought glitz to the luncheon, but the audience gave the event its electrifying power. As the 10th anniversary approached, Mercury News columnist Leigh Weimers called the affair "probably the Valley's prime networking party."

YWCA leaders, however, wanted more than a feminine – or even a feminist – network. They wanted to allow men on the board of directors, and they faced mounting community pressure to make that happen. In 1994, United Way asked the agencies it supported, including the YW, to pledge to end discrimination in programs, employment and on boards and committees. The YWCA served men as well as women. It had male employees, volunteers and advisers. But that was not enough. The association heard the message clearly: Recruit men to the governing board or risk losing critical dollars.

A Mercury News editorial chided United Way for "hassling" the YWCA, "one of its most valuable and effective member agencies." But the association's real conflict stood not with United Way so much as the national YWCA. San Jose women had lobbied for more than 20 years to include men on YW boards. But National refused.

In the days when men had controlled everything, the all-female board offered a rare chance for women to shine as leaders. That remained true in many communities, which was one reason why National stuck to its policy. But in late 20th century Santa Clara County, women had come to prominence. Witness the crowd at the YW's annual luncheon. In the '80s, the county earned a reputation as the feminist capital of the United States because so many women held powerful public office. A majority-female Board of Supervisors (including Wilson) had hired Sally Reed as the nation's first female executive of a metropolitan county, and women had held a majority on the San Jose City Council. During the United Way brouhaha, Susan Hammer was mayor. Women dominated non-profit boards, administered major social service agencies, ran large school districts, sat on city councils throughout the county, and increasingly, held top jobs in Silicon Valley companies, some of the richest, best-known corporations on the planet.

United Way eased up on the YW, but the association continued to fight National's ban. In the mid-1990s, San Jose and several other YWs petitioned the national association to permit male directors on an experimental basis. National rejected the proposal and threatened to disaffiliate any local that dared to break ranks.

YW women in San Jose had other problems with National – and they were not alone. Nearly 100 YWCAs closed from the late '70s through the '90s, one-quarter of the affiliates in the United States. With only 300 city YWs and six student groups still active, the YWCA of the USA listed fewer associations than at its founding in 1906. Local YW administrators bore at least some responsibility, because of lackluster programming and financial mismanagement. But with increasing anger, YW women throughout the country blamed the mother ship.

Community leaders complained, fairly or not, that New York headquarters had a bloated staff and executives who galloped the globe on humanitarian missions – yet seemed to devote little energy to the less glamorous work of helping community YWCAs stay relevant and solvent. Most galling, from the point of view of locals, they financed that neglect through hefty, sometimes crushing, dues. Many associations simply halted payments, an act of defiance that ranked, with adding men to the board, as grounds for disaffiliation. The San Jose board had stopped paying dues during the fund-raising drive for Villa Nueva – the directors had decided, reluctantly, to put the money into the building rather than send it to New York. As the association's budget soared, so did the annual dues assessment, until San Jose ran up a debt of about $250,000. The directors worried, end-

Steve Tedesco, CEO of the Boys & Girls Clubs of Silicon Valley, and Mark Walker, CEO of United Way Silicon Valley, wore high heels for Walk A Mile In Her Shoes in 2004. The annual walk raises awareness about sexual assault.

lessly, about the bill. They quietly considered dropping the YWCA name before National could rip it away.

But the standoff never came to that, because locals nationwide revolted in the late 1990s. They elected all new national leaders and set in motion the biggest overhaul in the YWCA of the USA in nearly a century. By the early 2000s, an unrecognizably lean national staff had moved to Washington, D.C. The national office focused on advocacy for what it called its "hallmark" issues – empowering women and eliminating racism – and promoting the YWCA "brand." For the first time, the YWCA movement in the United States ran from the ground up. City YWs supported and governed regional associations, and received training, management advice and financial guidance in return. (Under the new structure, San Jose's unpaid dues were forgiven.) The hemorrhaging slowed, although it did not stop. Among the YWs that died after the reorganization was the 52-year-old Mid-Peninsula YWCA, in Palo Alto, in June 2003.

Although the national YW – renamed YWCA USA in 2004 – kept the old prohibition against men, it eased the threat of punishment for renegades. On Oct. 25, 2004, the San Jose YW – renamed the YWCA of Silicon Valley earlier that year – became one of the first in the country to welcome men to the board of directors. Eager to avoid the taint of tokenism, the YWCA elected six men to the 24-member board: media executive Brian Adams, attorney Lon Allan, builder Steven G. Delva, winemaker Bill Murphy, commercial real estate consultant Michael L. Rosendin, and the county tax assessor, Larry Stone.

For YW women in San Jose, that election marked the sweetest triumph since the opening of Villa Nueva in 1993 and seemed to complete a significant shift. When the YW cut the ribbon on the building, it slashed a barrier that had kept the association – perhaps mostly in its own mind – on the sidelines of civic enterprise. Only six months after the building opened, Executive Director Linda Kibler told the board: "Expanded community visibility, which Villa Nueva has brought us, is becoming a reality." In 2004, at last, everyone could take part in the YWCA, at every level.

That the Susanne B. Wilson Residence had shaped up differently from the YWCA's dream cast a bittersweet tinge for some YW women. Many of the tenants stayed years longer than expected and few took advantage of the counseling, child care or classes downstairs. Still, the residence had evolved into a kind of community – by 2004, it had a large population of refugees from war-torn Eritrea and Ethiopia – and housing advocates continued to applaud the YW women who got it built. "They had incredible vision," said Carol J. Galante, president and CEO of Bridge Housing Corp. "They contributed back to the community." Alex Sanchez, executive director of the Santa Clara County Housing Authority and a longtime member of the YW advisory board, agreed. Villa Nueva, he said, "had a very positive effect."

YW women, especially those who had once felt the project flow through their veins, occasionally – and privately – expressed disappointment that tenants weren't primarily younger women and single-parent families on their way to better lives, using the YWCA to help them get there. But nobody at the YW had regrets. They had brought desperately needed housing to low-income families. And increasingly, the YWCA was all about helping the desperate.

The heart and soul of the YW, had, of course, always lain in the troubled recesses of the community. In 1905, when Harriet Cory formed the tiny association, she declared two immediate goals: hire a matron to aid young women arriving at the train depot friendless, and guarantee them fresh sheets in immaculate bedrooms in a cheerful, protective home. In the early

1920s, journalist Edith Daley wrote "The residence floor of the YWCA is a good place to go for a visit when you begin to feel there's not much real unselfishness in the world."

Daley went on to tell the florid tale of a "sullenly defiant" girl hauled in by the proprietor of a rooming house where she had stayed. "Lock her up," he ordered the YWCA housemother. "Lock her up so she can't go to that dance in the city tonight." But even in its sternest piety, the YWCA did not lock up girls. So to the dance she went, Daley reported, in a "tawdry little dress."

The girl returned past midnight and, to her surprise, found the matron brimming with concern. In the weeks that followed, the woman showered the girl with love and found a doctor who removed her tonsils and adenoids. "The physical relief unfettered the spirit," Daley wrote. The matron also tracked down the boy who had broken the girl's heart, spurring her to run away, and nudged the couple to reunite. "And their love story developed under motherly care and guidance – until the day came when they married," Daley reported. "And they're going to live happily ever after. We know they are, because that girl will never be able to forget or get away from the influence that caught her, and held her, and helped her to become the woman God meant her to be.

"Tip your hat to that building that wears the Blue Triangle...The most wonderful thing in the world is saving girls."

The details of the story may seem laughably, if not dubiously, overwrought. But its basic rhythm pulsed through the century. Goodwin Steinberg, whose firm designed Villa Nueva and the small administrative building that preceded it, first encountered the YWCA in the early '60s, after an acquaintance slit her wrists. Hers was a common story of the era: educated, married, new in town, stuck in the suburbs day after day, without a car or a nearby friend. She survived the suicide attempt and Steinberg called around for help. He heard about the YWCA, "an answer that just made my ears perk up," he recalled. It had classes, child care and best of all, women happy to swing by in their station wagons and give his acquaintance a lift. He credited the YWCA with saving her life.

Kimberly Isom credited the YWCA with saving her sanity. In May 2003, Isom was kidnapped and raped by two men in Los Angeles. She returned home to San Jose two weeks later, and thought, with growing panic, that she was losing her mind. She felt terrified to go out or stay home. She fought with her family and sobbed with loneliness. She could not drag herself from bed. She hurt just to breathe. She called the Rape Crisis Center, and over

Sandy Davis, director of the Rape Crisis Center, and San Jose Police Chief Rob Davis (no relation) at Walk a Mile in Her Shoes in 2004.

weeks, then months, a counselor helped her see that her anguish, fear and fury were normal, not signs of lunacy or punishment for the savage attack. That wisdom and support "meant everything for my recovery," Isom said. "I'll be recovering for the rest of my life, but I don't know that I'd even be this functional if it hadn't been for the YW."

For much of its history, however, the association's dedication to service was part of a broader endeavor. The YWCA sought to forge a band of women who would use their collective muscle to improve not only their own lives but also the world. From the Bible circles of Harriet Cory's day, to the Depression-era clubs for shop clerks, to the jitterbugging Hi-Spot of World War II, to the racial dialogues and worry clinics of the late '60s and '70s, the YWCA held itself to be not merely an organization but a movement. Members sat in classes and taught them. Members joined clubs and led them. Over time, members molded an enterprise unlike any other: a rich, almost indefinable mix of activities, from winsome to weighty to groundbreaking.

By the 1990s, the YWCA had evolved into a human service organization. Although volunteers still played a strong role as parent-educators, rape counselors and fund-raisers, professionals designed and closely supervised the programs. Keri Procunier McLain, a former nun, hospital administrator and Santa Clara councilmember, became CEO in April 1998, the first top executive to arrive with a doctorate (in organizational psychology) but no previous YW work experience. Increasingly, YW directors came not through the membership ranks and years of volunteer service, but through professional and civic connections.

The new guard lacked the crusading edge of old. But the board and staff had a passion for helping women, children and families, along with considerable fund-raising contacts and skill. In the golden Silicon Valley economy of the 1990s, donations and grants seemed to rain down. The YWCA used them to create one innovative program after another.

Next Step offered yearlong workshops, and an alternative to Juvenile Hall, for teen-agers sent by judges for drug-related crimes and truancy. (Judge Leonard Edwards – grandson and namesake of the civic leader who had saved the association from foreclosure in the 1940s – spearheaded the partnership between Juvenile Court and the YW.) The sessions covered the gamut, from communication skills and anger management to work ethic and career planning. New Options, modeled on a national program to reduce teen pregnancy, ran daily after-school sessions at high schools in East San Jose, starting at William C. Overfelt, which had one of the highest pregnancy rates in California. Group leaders provided homework help, mentoring, college counseling and workshops on health, safe sex and drug and alcohol abuse – all to instill a sense of possibility in young people who saw only dead ends.

Kids' Connection worked with families torn by custody battles. Parent education programs served parents of children of every age, parents with special-needs children, grandparents raising kids and parents referred by social workers because of child abuse or neglect.

The YW set up wintertime child care and classes for mothers from the San Jose Family Shelter, because shelters shut during the day and forced residents outside no matter how cold or rainy the weather. The Rape Crisis Center spawned a long-term counseling service after the staff realized that the emotional wounds of sexual assault take months or years to heal – sometimes, even to surface. The center also launched Teen Empowerment, to teach sixth- through 12th-graders how to recognize, repel and report sexual assault. About 3,600 students took classes the first year. When asked what they had learned, kids replied with aching simplicity: "How not to be afraid to say no." "No matter what happens, rape is not your fault." "We learned to have confidence in ourselves and be proud of who we are."

In late 2000, the Silicon Valley economy soured and had yet to recover fully more than four years later. As donations and grants dried up, the YW spun off some services and closed others, including the Employment Center and five child-care sites. But the most successful programs continued to grow. Rape Crisis, directed by Sandy Davis, extended counseling and advocacy to north Santa Clara County, filling a gap left by the closure of the Mid-Peninsula YWCA. The hotline logged more than 1,000 assault reports a year. In the rare instance that a rape case went to court without a YWCA advocate, the district attorney would call one, and even reschedule the hearing so an advocate could attend. It marked a stunning turnaround from the early years, when Rape Crisis clawed its way into a legal system ignorant about, and largely indifferent to, sexual violence.

Parent education programs, under Stacy Castle, also expanded to Palo Alto. New Options, directed by Graciela Valladares, moved into middle schools. The counseling service, initially for rape survivors, developed into a full counseling center, under Mary Diridon. It sent counselors into middle and high schools, after budget cuts forced San Jose Unified to lay off staff counselors and social workers. The center also provided low-cost treatment, in Spanish and English, for depression, anxiety, grief, behavior problems and family conflict, and ran support groups, including one for new fathers and another for high-tech women who had given up careers to stay home with their babies.

In so many obvious ways, the YWCA of 2005 had traveled light years from its origins. The old champion of women workers was now helping young professionals find fulfillment in changing diapers. The moralist that once forbade coed dancing was now handing out condoms in public schools. At 4 p.m. on a Monday in January 1906, Miss Agnes Howe of the San Jose Normal School attended a devotional meeting at the YWCA. At 4 p.m. on a Wednesday in January 2005, Sophia Hernandez, a senior at Mount Pleasant High in East San Jose, attended a YWCA college workshop. From prayer to pregnancy prevention, from the pious Harriet Cory to the passionate Keri Procunier McLain, the YW had changed as remarkably as the lives of the women it served.

Yet at heart, the YWCA had not changed much at all. It still held the optimistic faith that every person has value and the capacity for growth. It still believed that by working together, people accomplish what nobody can alone – for themselves, for one another and for us all. At 100, the old lady remained the fierce idealist of her youth – never mind that her latest customers looked nothing remotely like her first. Through a century of classes, clubs and crusades, she gave everyone the same gifts: the opportunity to choose their destiny, and the power to shape it.

At the YWCA today, a woman makes peace with her decision to quit a powerful, high-paying job to stay home with her kids. Another woman leaves her toddler at the child-care center and zips off to work. Kimberly Isom volunteers for the Rape Crisis Center, mustering strength she once believed she had lost to sit in the hospital and whisper calming words to women who have just been brutalized. And Sophia Hernandez hears five afternoons a week, from adults she trusts, that she can make choices that will move her toward everything she wants in life. One day, her group leader skips the serious talk and, in that enduring YWCA spirit, hauls out crafts. Sophia and her friends make dream-catchers.

Arthur Murray YWCA dance class in the summer of 1954. All eyes watched the

feet of teachers Desiree Moralez and William Davis.

AFTERWORD

As you have read, the story of the YWCA is about dedication and commitment. It is the story of a mission – to empower women, children and their families; and to eliminate racism, hatred and prejudice. Most importantly, it is a story of individuals – the staff, volunteers and donors who have helped improve so many lives over the past 100 years in this place now called Silicon Valley.

The YWCA provided services to more than 26,000 people in 2004, most of them children and teens. But statistics do not begin to reflect what happens inside the YWCA. Staff members offer more than just programs. One worker, unable to find immediate shelter for a victim of sexual abuse, invited the terrified woman into her home. The woman is now safe in her own residence, working and volunteering for the YWCA. Another employee heard that two young clients could not afford dresses for their senior prom. She and her colleagues dug deep to send the two thrilled girls off in style.

Volunteers are equally generous and resourceful. Whether mentoring a young person, serving on a board or committee, clerking in the office or building a bookshelf, our volunteers give hours and days to make a difference. Sometimes, those hours come in the middle of the night. For 32 years, the rape crisis hotline has been staffed around the clock. That reassuring voice on the phone probably is a volunteer; so is the person who accompanies a victim to the hospital, then turns around and goes to work the next morning.

Many YW supporters aid financially, with donations large and small. Their contributions help sustain programs to educate parents and to help young people make responsible choices.

As in the past, the YWCA will face challenges that sometimes seem overwhelming. But now we have a written history that reminds us of our courage and our accomplishments. Each one of us – employee, volunteer and donor – is a part of that history. Each of us is the heart and soul of the YWCA today, as well as a source of strength for its future.

Keri Procunier McLain

*"Many small people in many small
places doing many small things
can alter the face of the Earth."*

Message scratched onto the Berlin Wall

I

Milestones Through the Century

1905   YWCA is organized in San Jose. Headquarters and women's residence open on East St. James Street.

1906   The San Jose association becomes a charter member of the Young Women's Christian Associations of the United States of America.

1914   YWCA of Santa Clara Valley incorporates.

1916   YWCA building, designed by Julia Morgan, opens at South Second and San Antonio streets. With an indoor pool, gymnasium, assembly hall, small residence, cafeteria and parlors, the three-story building is San Jose's first community center for women.

1917   YWCA organizes major fund-raising drive for war relief. The effort leads to the creation of the Women's Mobilized Army of Santa Clara County.

1918   YWCA establishes Girl Reserves, providing organized activities and leadership development for 12- to 18-year olds.

1920   After the ratification of the 19th Amendment, guaranteeing women the right to vote, YWCA offers classes in democracy and the responsibilities of citizenship.

1923   YWCA participates in the founding of the Community Chest, forerunner to United Way.

1926   YWCA opens a four-story annex adjacent to the original building.

1930   YWCA expands services for working women, with vocational counseling, classes, clubs and the Business Girls' League.

1941   National YWCA participates in the creation of USO. The San Jose association organizes dances in San Jose and at area military bases.

1944   The Hi-Spot for teens opens in the YWCA basement, and becomes a wildly popular hangout and a model for youth leadership programs.

1947   The first YWCA nursery provides baby-sitting so mothers can attend a wives' club.

1949   YWCA launches Ladies' Day Out, accelerating a shift toward programs for suburban housewives.

1956   The YWCA offers Ladies' Day Out in San Jose's Cambrian district, the first step in decentralization.

1964   YWCA establishes its first satellite, Cambrian Center, later known as YWCA-West Valley.

1967   Working with San Jose Unified School District, YWCA launches the Young Mothers Program, the first high school classes for pregnant teens.

1969   San Jose representatives participate in the Racial Justice Institute in Palo Alto, the first of eight meetings organized by the national YWCA to consider the organization's response to racism in America.

1970   National convention unanimously adopts the YWCA's One Imperative to eliminate racism "by any means necessary." San Jose YWCA launches classes for children in ethnicity and multiculturalism and expands programs in East San Jose.

1971   YWCA Racial Justice Committee publishes a directory of black-owned businesses in San Jose.

1973   YWCA sells the building to the San Jose Redevelopment Agency. It is razed for San Antonio Plaza Urban Renewal.

1973   YWCA launches 24-hour rape crisis hotline, the first in Santa Clara County and only the second in California.

1975   YWCA administrative building opens at 375 S. Third Street.

1978   YW launches the Hispanic Program and expands outreach to Spanish-speaking women, children and families.

1985   San Jose hosts the 30th National YWCA Convention. More than 1,200 delegates attend. The local association also holds first TWIN, Tribute to Women and Industry, to salute business, professional and managerial achievement.

1991   YWCA holds first Professional Women's Luncheon. Nearly 1,000 people attend.

1993   Villa Nueva opens. The five-story complex contains YWCA offices, a child-care center and 63 low-cost apartments.

2004   Six men join the YWCA Board of Directors. The association is renamed YWCA of Silicon Valley.

2005   YWCA celebrates 100 years of service.

Recruitment poster for the YWCA Girl Reserves.

II

YWCA Leaders: 1905 ~ 2005

From General Secretary to CEO

1906	Elizabeth Porter
1907-10	Chloe Case Anderson
1910	Irene H. Moule
1916-19	Ada B. Hillman
1919-23	Emma Palmer
1923-25	Mrs. W.M. Case
1926-40	Patricia Davidson
1940-47	Edna Pearce
1947-49	Elizabeth MacDonald
1950-59	Elizabeth Blaisdell
1959	Mrs. John E. Cooper
1959-77	Lois M. Cullison
1977-83	Jan Vandervest
1983-93	Faith Rein
1993-95	Linda Kibler
1995-97	Katherine H. Toch
1998-	Keri Procunier McLain

Board Presidents

1905-06	Harriet Cory
1907-08	Laura Chapin Bailey

1909	Edith Cory Alexander
1910	Mrs. Alex Martha Murgotten
1914	Mrs. David A. (Agnes) Beattie
1915	Mrs. J.B.T. Tuthill
1916-17	Mrs. Charles B. Hare
1918	Mrs. Lou T. (Iva) Smith
1919-20	Mrs. Claude O. (Georgia) Winans
1921-22	Mrs. David A. (Agnes) Beattie
1923-24	Mrs. Robert Vickery
1924	Mrs. G.H. McMurry
1925	Mrs. W.L. Chandler
1926	Mrs. Wesley Toy
1927-28	Mrs. James (Alice) DeVoss
1929-30	Mrs. Lou T. (Iva) Smith
1931-32	Mrs. Forest L. Burch
1933-34	Mrs. E.M. Jefferson
1935-36	Mrs. Guy W. (Grace) Smith
1937-39	Mrs. Maude E. Empey
1940-41	Mrs. W.H. Bostwick
1942-43	Mrs. Luther Wool
1944	Mrs. Forrest Murdock
1945-46	Mrs. Christopher (Margaret) Nedderson
1947-48	Mrs. J.H. Harcourt
1949-50	Mrs. Chester (Mary) Root
1951-52	Dr. Ruth Landon
1953-54	Miss Margaret Chase
1955-56	Mrs. Harold (Evelyn) Wellington
1957	Mrs. C.H. McManus Jr.
1958-59	Mrs. J.H. Wythe
1959-60	Mrs. Chester (Mary) Root
1961-62	Mrs. Izetta Pritchard
1963-65	Lucille Wright
1965-66	Florence Stahl
1966-67	Fern Topham
1967-70	Susanne B. Wilson
1970-73	Mae H. Dailey

1973-76	Inez Jackson
1976-77	Diana Larson
1977-79	Dorothy Anderson
1980-81	Helen Hayashi
1981-82	Annette Suth
1982-83	Mary Katherine Kelley
1983-85	Sarah Janigian
1985-87	Joleen Callahan
1987- 88	Jenifer Williams
1988-91	Sarah Janigian
1991-93	Pamela Bogle
1993-95	Jacquelyn Lauer
1995-97	Katie Sween
1997-99	Chris DiSalvo
1999-2001	Jill Arnone
2001-03	Mary E. Morris
2003-	Brenda Komar

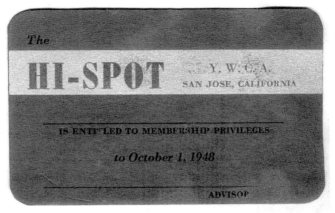

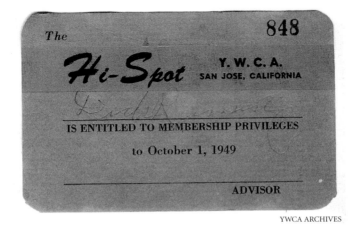

Hi-Spot membership cards.

III

YWCA Board of Directors
2005~06

President	**Brenda Komar**
1st Vice President	**Helen Hayashi**
2nd Vice President	**Jennifer M. George**
Treasurer	**Connie Tritt**
Secretary	**Edesa Bitbadal**

Brian Adams
Lon Allan
Teresa Alvarado
Debbie Blackwell
Elizabeth Bliss
Joleen Callahan
Charlotte D. Chang
Joan Cloughesy
Mary Jean Connors
Theresa Dadone-Carlsted
Steven G. Delva
Andrea J. Elliott
Gloria Mink Edwards
Mary E. Morris
Bill Murphy
Michael L. Rosendin
Eileen Schloss
Larry Stone
Nga Trinh-Halperin

Chief Executive Officer	**Keri Procunier McLain**

THE GOLDEN JUBILEE
and Every Girl Reserve Festivity
will prove immensely captivating
and fascinating if graced by the

NEW GIRL RESERVE DRESS

PRICE $2.35 Without Tie
Tie With "G. R." Monogram 25c additional

An early advertisement for a Girl Reserve uniform. The tie cost extra.

A YWCA guest book cover from 1917, made from leather and cloth.

BIBLIOGRAPHY

YWCA: Books, Pamphlets and Reports

Asilomar: The First Fifty Years 1913-1963. Asilomar Conference Grounds.

Black, Winifred. *The Life and Personality of Phoebe Apperson Hearst.* San Simeon: Friends of Hearst Castle, 1991.

Boutelle, Sara Holmes. *Julia Morgan, Architect.* New York: Abbeville Press, 1988.

Boyd, Nancy. *Emissaries: The Overseas Work of the American YWCA 1895-1970.* New York: The Woman's Press, 1986.

Briesemeister, Esther. *America's Children: What Happened to Us? Report of the Japanese Evacuation Project. Jan. 1942-Sept. 1946.* New York: National Board of the YWCA, 1946.

Creedy, Brooks Spivey. *Women Behind the Lines: YWCA Program with War Production Workers, 1940-1947.* New York: The Woman's Press, 1949.

Calkins, Gladys Gilkey. *The Negro in the Young Women's Christian Association: A Study of the Development of YWCA Interracial Policies and Practices in their Historical Setting.* Master's thesis. Washington, D.C.: George Washington University, 1960.

Dodson, Dan W. *The Role of the YWCA in a Changing Era: The YWCA*

Study of YMCA-YWCA Cooperative Experiences. New York: National Board of the YWCA of the USA, 1960.

Dugid, Julian. *The Blue Triangle.* London: Hodder & Stoughton Ltd., 1955.

Hart, Wendy Allison. *Dedicated Toward Nobler Womanhood: Julia Morgan and the YWCA.* Master's thesis. Ithaca, N.Y.: Cornell University, 1991.

Hendee, Elizabeth Russell. *The Growth and Development of the Young Women's Christian Association.* New York: The Woman's Press, 1930.

Lerrigo, Edith M. *YWCA Purpose: Lodestar of the Movement.* New York: National Board of the YWCA, 1974.

Mains, Frances Helen and Elliott, Grace Loucks. *From Deep Roots: The Story of the YWCA's Religious Dimensions.* New York: National Board of the YWCA, 1974.

Rice, Anna V. *A History of the World's Young Women's Christian Association.* New York: The Woman's Press, 1947.

Robertson, Nancy M. *Deeper Than Race? White Women and the Politics of Christian Sisterhood in the Young Women's Christian Association.* Paper presented at American Historical Association meeting, Dec. 27-30, 1987.

Robinson, Marion O. *Eight Women of the YWCA.* New York: National Board of the YWCA, 1966.

Rumble, the Rev. Dr. L., MSC, *YMCA, YWCA: Not for Catholics.* St. Paul, Minn.: Radio Replies Press Society.

Sims, Mary S. *The First 25 Years.* New York: The Woman's Press, 1932.

Sims, Mary S. *The Natural History of a Social Institution: The YWCA.* New York: The Woman's Press, 1936.

Sims, Mary S. *The Place of the Young Women's Christian Association in Cities.* New York: The Woman's Press, 1930.

Wadsworth, Ginger. *Julia Morgan: Architect of Dreams*. Minneapolis: Lerner Publications Co., 1990.

Williamson, Margaret. *They Call Us a Group Work Agency*. New York: The Woman's Press, 1939.

Wilson, Grace H. *The Religious and Educational Philosophy of the Young Women's Christian Association*. New York: Bureau of Publications, Teachers College, Columbia University, 1933.

Young Women's Christian Association, National Board
   Annual Reports, YWCA of the USA, 1951-1992.
   National Convention Reports, 1906-1985.
   Thinking about the YWCA: Reflections by Women of the YWCA of the USA on the Occasion of the 100th Anniversary of the World YWCA. 1894-1994/5.
   Writings of Edith M. Lerrigo, compilation reprinted from *The YWCA Magazine*.
   Yearbooks and Statistical Directories, 1912-1916.

Women's History

Gullett, Gayle. *Becoming Citizens: The Emergence and Development of the California Women's Movement, 1880-1911*. Urbana: University of Illinois Press, 2000.

Jensen, Joan M. and Lothrop, Gloria Ricci. *California Women: A History*. San Francisco: Boyd & Fraser Publishing Co., 1987.

Immell, Myra H., editor. *The 1900s*. San Diego: Greenhaven Press, 2000.

Matthews, Glenna. *Silicon Valley, Women, and the California Dream: Gender, Class, and Opportunity in the Twentieth Century*. Stanford: Stanford University Press, 2003.

Ruiz, Vicki L., *Cannery Women, Cannery Lives: Mexican Women, Unionization, and the California Food Processing Industry, 1930-1950.* Albuquerque: University of New Mexico Press, 1987.

History of San Jose and the Santa Clara Valley

Arbuckle, Clyde. *Clyde Arbuckle's History of San Jose.* San Jose: Smith & McKay Printing Co., 1985.

Arbuckle, Helen; Arbuckle, Jim, editor. *San Jose's Women: Colonial Days to the 1970s.* San Jose: J. Arbuckle, 2002.

Beilharz, Edwin A. *San Jose: California's First City.* Tulsa: Continental Heritage Press, 1980.

Brockway, Edith. *San Jose Reflections: An Illustrated History of San Jose, California, and Some of the Surrounding Area.* Campbell: Academy Press, 1977.

Cunningham, Florence R.; Fox, Frances L., editor. *Saratoga's First Hundred Years.* San Jose: 1967.

Daley, Edith. *War History of Santa Clara County.* San Jose: Santa Clara County Historical Society, 1919.

Douglas, John R. *Historical Footnotes of Santa Clara Valley.* San Jose: San Jose Historical Museum Association, 1993.

Farrell, Harry. *San Jose – and Other Famous Places.* San Jose: San Jose Historical Museum Association, 1983.

Farrell, Harry. *Swift Justice: Murder and Vengeance in a California Town.* New York: St. Martin's Press, 1992.

Foote, H.S., editor. *Pen Pictures from the Garden of the World, or Santa Clara County, California.* Chicago: Lewis Publishing, 1960.

Garden City Women's Club (San Jose). *History of Black Americans in Santa Clara Valley*. Sunnyvale: Lockheed Missiles & Space Co., 1978.

Gilbert, Levi. *The Hundred Year History of YMCA in San Jose and Santa Clara Valley*. San Jose: YMCA of Santa Clara Valley, 1967.

Gilbert, Lauren Miranda and Johnson, Bob. *San Jose's Historic Downtown*, Charleston, S.C.: Arcadia Publishing, 2004.

Greathead, Sarah Estelle Hammond. *The Story of an Inspiring Past: Historical Sketch of the San Jose State Teachers College from 1862 to 1928*. San Jose: San Jose State Teachers College, 1928.

Ignoffo, Mary Jo. *A Meeting of the Minds: A Retrospective of the To Kalon Club of San Jose, Calif., 1903-2003*. Cupertino: California History Center & Foundation, 2002.

Peck, Willys I. *The How and "Y" of it: 125 years of the YMCA in Santa Clara Valley*. San Jose: YMCA of Santa Clara Valley, 1992.

Reflections of the Past: an anthology of San Jose. Encinitas, Calif.: Heritage Media Corp., 1996.

Sawyer, Eugene T., *History of Santa Clara County, California*. Los Angeles: Historic Record Co., 1922.

Trounstine, Philip J. and Christensen, Terry. *Movers and Shakers: The Study of Community Power*. New York: St. Martin's Press, 1982.

*Cover of a Y-Teens newsletter. YWCA members were never shy about
waving the banner of their clubs and their association.*

INDEX